A Labyrinth Year

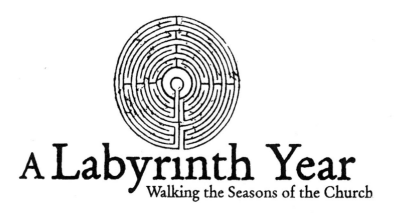

A Labyrinth Year
Walking the Seasons of the Church

Richard Kautz

Morehouse Publishing
NEW YORK · HARRISBURG · DENVER

Morehouse Publishing, 4775 Linglestown Road, Harrisburg, PA 17112

Morehouse Publishing, 445 Fifth Avenue, New York, NY 10016

Morehouse Publishing is an imprint of Church Publishing Incorporated.
www.churchpublishing.org

Library of Congress Cataloging-in-Publication Data
Kautz, Richard A.
  A labyrinth year : walking the seasons of the church / Richard A. Kautz.
    p. cm.
  ISBN 978-0-8192-2157-5 (pbk.)
  1. Church year meditations. 2. Bible--Devotional use. 3. Labyrinths--Religious aspects--Christianity. I. Title.
  BV30.K35 2005
  242'.3--dc22
                    2005004739

Printed in the United States of America

To my wonderful kids
Ron, Stephanie, and Jessica.
Thanks for putting up with your crazy dad.
I love you with all my heart.

Contents

Acknowledgments

I would like to start by thanking the "Bad Girls" of the Thursday morning women's bible study at Trinity Episcopal Church in Greeley, Colorado. I began this book as an Advent bible study based on the labyrinth. After we finished the class, this group encouraged me to look into having it published. Without their loving support and gentle nudging, this book would never have been published.

Before I sent the original manuscript off to a publisher, I had two friends from Trinity go over the document with a fine tooth comb. A special thanks to Helen Lonsdale and Deirdre White-Jones for their expertise in grammar and language. Their comments were both helpful and encouraging.

When Morehouse asked me to expand the book to include the full Church calendar, I knew I couldn't face the task on my own. I asked Helen once again if she would help me. She agreed and kept plugging through my writing even during a brief health crisis. Thank you from the bottom of my heart, Helen. You were a Godsend and I could not have done it without you.

I want to thank Nancy Fitzgerald at Morehouse Publishing. Nancy, you were loving and gentle with this first-time author. Thank you for your ideas and comments. Your polish really shines through.

Last, and not least, I want to thank my family. They supported me through a lot of personal growth and change. You helped make me who I am. Thank your for your love throughout the years. I love you.

Introduction

The Journey

Deep within all people and in every culture is knowledge of the great journey. Call it a quest, or an odyssey, or the great adventure: you'll find it in children's stories, songs, art, literature, and—in modern times—in movies and on television.

The Bible is a collection of stories of God's people on a journey. The journey began when Adam and Eve were expelled from the garden. Our first parents had lived fully in God's presence, walking and talking with their creator. "Gender exclusive" is fine in the cool shade of paradise. But when sin entered into paradise, humankind was driven out of the presence of God. Since that moment, all of us have been on a journey back to Eden, on an eager walk back to God. St. Augustine of Hippo wrote, "Our heart is restless, until it rests in Thee."

For the Church, this journey, taking on a special meaning, has become a pilgrimage. The practice of pilgrimage is common to most religions. Hindus travel to Benares, the holiest site in India. Muslims are to make at least one pilgrimage to Mecca in their lifetime. Jews as well as Christians travel to Jerusalem. The practice of the Christian pilgrimage to the Holy Land started in the fourth century CE, when Helena, mother of the emperor Constantine, visited Jerusalem and traced the steps of Christ on his way to the cross.

Today a pilgrimage is any journey we take to a holy place as an act of devotion, thanksgiving, or penance, or in search of a healing. Christian pilgrimage sites are spread across the globe, from Lourdes, to Chartres in France, to Medjugorje in Bosnia, to Our Lady of Walsingham in England, and to sites as far away as Mt. Sinai in Egypt and the shrine of Guadalupe in Mexico. But as important as the destination is the process of the journey itself. As people of the Incarnation—disciples of Jesus, who is God-made-flesh—we somehow need to "flesh out" what is happening to us spiritually. Historically, primarily Catholics, Orthodox, and Anglicans—members of churches that identify themselves as sacramental—have sensed the importance of making an outwardly visible sign of God's invisible spiritual grace through an act of pilgrimage. But Christians from all denominations are beginning to connect with their need for an outward pilgrimage that mirrors their inward journey. In the words of St. Augustine, "It is solved by walking."

The Labyrinth

Almost as ancient as the pilgrimage itself is the symbolic journey of the labyrinth. Dating back more than four thousand years, the oldest European labyrinth, known as the classic seven-circuit variety, was found on the island of Crete. Labyrinths are found in a variety of belief structures, from Judaism to Native American religions, and in countries like England, Scandinavia, Germany, and the Americas. Some labyrinths, laid out in gardens and fields and in the floors of temples and great cathedrals, were designed to be walked—the earliest and most famous of these is in the nave of Chartres Cathedral in France. Smaller images of labyrinths, intended strictly for meditation, were placed in paintings, sculptures, and tapestries. But whether the labyrinths are used for mental or physical meditation, they express humanity's quest for something more. They help us get in touch with the great journey buried in our hearts.

The labyrinth takes us on a journey that brings us to the very center of our being—and back out again. Unlike a maze, which is designed to keep us lost or confused, a labyrinth is designed to help us find our way to our core. And even when we've reached it, our journey is not complete. It's only half over. We're not to just walk away, but to retrace our steps back out to complete the full cycle.

The labyrinth, neither inherently Christian nor non-Christian, has been adapted to our faith tradition in the same way that symbols like the Advent wreath and the Christmas tree began as pagan practices and were later "baptized" by the Church and infused with Christian meaning. A labyrinth is merely a tool that helps us bring a spiritual reality into a tangible experience. In the pages of this book, seekers will discover a labyrinth journey that takes them through the seasons of the Church year.

How to Use the Meditations in This Book

The Church calendar is made up of commemorations and feasts for specific Holy Days such as Christmas, Ash Wednesday, and Easter Sunday. The calendar also divides the year into six seasons: Advent, Christmas, Epiphany, Lent, Eastertide, and the Sundays after Pentecost, normally called Ordinary Time. The seasons roughly coincide with the life and ministry of Jesus.

The Church year begins with the expectation of the coming of the Christ Child, Advent. Christmas continues with the birth narratives up until the Feast of the Epiphany. Epiphany links the birth narratives with the manifestation of Jesus as Emmanuel, God with us. Sundays during the season of Epiphany bring us lessons showing that Jesus is indeed God made flesh. Lent allows us to participate in

Christ's journey to the cross. During Easter we hear of Jesus' resurrection appearances culminating in the Feast of the Ascension. At Pentecost we remember the promised arrival of the Holy Spirit. During the season after Pentecost, we follow the teachings and parables of Christ through one of the three Synoptic Gospels. Taken together, the seasons of the Church year provide a journey through the life of Christ, beginning with waiting for the birth of a tiny King of the Jews in a manger and ending with Christ reigning at the right hand of the Father in the Feast of Christ the King.

These labyrinth meditations are taken from Sunday readings throughout the Church year. They are accounts of individuals who met Jesus on the road and how that encounter changed them. Each personal encounter is comprised of two or more meditations. First is the encounter itself. Next is the person's walk back into their world after being transformed by coming face to face with God. Hopefully you will find something in their journey that touches you in yours. If you have access to a labyrinth, great! If not, don't let that stop you. Find a park or a trail or any makeshift path. The point is to get moving. Prayer walking is a great way to connect to God and creation. If you can't get outside, use a finger labyrinth to give you a sense of movement even indoors, as you let your finger trace the path while you pray the meditations. You can purchase finger labyrinths made of metal or wood, or you can even make your own (see page 107 for a pattern).

The meditations in this book were originally designed for use in a Bible study class. After participants made their own finger labyrinths using fabric and fabric paint, I read the meditations aloud slowly, with many pauses for quiet reflection. The class would sit quietly and listen as they traced their fingers along the cloth pathway in front of them. For our last class, we went to a local church that had a permanent labyrinth in its floor. The entire group of ten people was able to walk the labyrinth slowly as I read three meditations aloud. If you wish to use these meditations in a group setting, I suggest you have one person read the meditations while others follow along, or you may tape the meditations so that everyone can walk and no one is left out.

An important consideration in using these meditations is the number of them you do at one time. I can't stress enough: take your time. A labyrinth experience shouldn't be hurried or rushed. You can use several meditations, perhaps an entire movement, during the course of one labyrinth walk, or you may want to take one meditation at a time. If you're reading these meditations as you walk, I suggest you walk for a short bit, pause and read a portion of the meditation, then begin walking again. Depending on what I've just read, there are times I prefer to be still as I meditate, and other times when I prefer to be moving as I integrate the words into my heart. There is no correct way to walk a labyrinth or to use this book. It is your pilgrimage. Listen to your inner rhythm and let that be your best guide.

You are now ready to begin your pilgrimage. Prepare your mind and open your heart to the presence of God. Put all your trust in God, who will lead you where you need to go.

The First Movement: Walking to Bethlehem

Advent/Christmas

THE CALL

Mary (Luke 1:26–38)

God's call never comes in a time or manner you'd expect. You can't prepare for it or request that it arrive on a certain day or at a specific moment. God is the caller; you are the receiver. It matters little to God whether you're deep in prayer or busy with ordinary tasks. When God extends a hand to you, it's in God's time, not yours.

That's how it happened with Mary. By all accounts, she was a young girl. In our culture, she seems too young to be thinking of marriage, of building a home, of having children. In our day, we'd see her in that awkward stage between dolls and dates. But in her world she was doing exactly what was expected of her—preparing to be a bride. Barely in her teens, she had her future all laid out for her. Her family had made the arrangements and she was betrothed to a good man. She would obey her parents' wishes, marry her betrothed, raise his children, and make a home for her new family. But God had other plans.

Scripture doesn't mention where or when the angel Gabriel came to Mary. Was it in the cool of the evening or in the hot midday sun? Was she going about her daily chores—fetching water, sweeping the floor—or was she kneeling in quiet prayer? We don't know, nor do we need to. If we knew exactly what she was doing at that precise moment, we might tend to make that our focus. We might say, "*That's how we must encounter God.*" But the point isn't *how* Mary heard God—or even how we go about hearing God. It's about God's leading and our being obedient. It's about God's initiative, God's action. Mary's response—and ours—should be simply: "Here I am, the servant of the Lord; let it be with me according to your word."

Your Advent journey also begins with a call. Some legends of Mary speak of a dove that always appeared in those special moments. As you shop for presents, send cards to family and friends, and wander the congested malls and supermarkets, be on guard for the unexpected brilliance of angels. The sheer power of the moment may take your breath away. In your excitement tinged with terror, God's voice may have to comfort you with those same words the angel spoke to Mary: "Be not afraid."

But then again, God's voice may be found in the soft fluttering of a dove. A fluttering so soft and delicate that, if you aren't paying attention, you could miss it altogether. You may be caught up in glorious worship, surrounded by the sights, sounds, and smells of church. Or you may be right in the midst of the drab, ordinary stuff of life. Whatever the circumstances and wherever you may be, God is calling you to the highest of callings, asking you to carry the Son. God is calling you to be pregnant with the Holy Spirit. God is calling you to put aside all the plans the world has for you and to follow a different plan. Are you ready to begin your journey? How obedient are you right now? Are you ready to say, "Here I am, Lord. Use me."

Joseph (Matthew 1:19–25)

We know exactly where Joseph was when he heard the call: he was in bed, asleep. There were no flashes of light, no tangible being that he could reach out and touch, not even an opportunity to ask questions. There was just a dream in the night.

We know very little about Joseph. He was a carpenter and a descendant of the family of David. That's it. We do get to see his actions, and they speak to the kind of man he was. He knew what was right and how things needed to be done. His training as a carpenter taught him that. In construction, things fit together just so, and Joseph may have seen life in much the same way. He knew the law and what it meant for Mary to be carrying a child that wasn't his. She could have been stoned to death for adultery. But the Bible tells us that Joseph was a righteous man and unwilling to expose Mary to such a fate. It says he resolved to end the betrothal, send her away, and spare her. It wasn't an easy decision. He cared for Mary. Should he marry her anyway? Should he follow the law and expose her to harm? The Bible indicates that he weighed all the options and decided to do the right thing. With the hard decision behind him, Joseph went to bed, dreading the difficult task that awaited him. Into that fitful night's sleep, God sent his angel.

Sometimes we get a dramatic sign of God's will for us. Sometimes we have a dream that seems so right that we know just what to do when we awake. Mary was obedient to God's call. So was Joseph, but somehow his response seems to us to come more out of duty. Everyone hears God in different ways. Even the same person may not always hear God in the same way each time. Reflect on those times of call when you didn't get a tangible sign. Reflect on the quiet moments of God's presence when you just "knew" what was right. Trust in God to lead you where you need to go—and don't always ask for a sign. If your heart is grounded in the will of God, it will know the sound of God's voice.

The Magi (Matthew 2:1–8)

The call came to the magi long before the Word was made flesh in Mary's womb. Their study told them that a great celestial sign would accompany the birth of a new king, a king unlike any other. They were from a different land, a different culture, a different religion. They were kingly advisors, prophets, priests, magicians, and scientists. They didn't answer the call out of obedience or duty. They were searching for truth. They were drawn because they sensed something awesome and wondrous.

We tend to limit God and want God to act according to our expectations: God should be predictable, logical, and stick to the rules. God calls people like Mary and Joseph—respectable, religious people, not the unrighteous. That would be like throwing pearls before swine. We look around our churches and single out those individuals who seem so holy, so kind, so nice, and we say to ourselves, "God has a hand on them!" And it's true! But it often seems that God likes to use another kind of individual as well. God has a penchant for calling the wild ones: one with a hair shirt and a diet of locusts and wild honey, a persecutor who kills the faithful, even a trio of pagan magicians. God can call anyone, and the person is not always someone we expect. God is constantly turning our world upside down. Mary proclaimed it in her Magnificat: "He has shown strength with His arm; he has scattered the proud in the thoughts of their hearts. He has brought down the powerful from their thrones, and lifted up the lowly; he has filled the hungry with good things, and sent the rich away empty."

As you begin your journey to Bethlehem, think about being an outsider. You leave what is familiar and head out to someplace unknown, all because you hope for something wonderful. Into the night you go, with only a star to guide you. You don't know what you will find. You just know that you have to go because whatever it is, it's worth it, and it will turn your world upside down.

The Road

Mary (Luke 2:1–7)

It had been almost nine months since the angel gave Mary the miraculous news. She'd done everything God had asked of her. Now, with the baby due any day, she had to travel to Bethlehem. Why now? Why this arduous journey at such an inopportune time? Wasn't it enough to give birth to the Son of God without having to travel ninety miles on foot and donkey? The birth of a child was a family event—all the women would gather around to help bring a new life into the world. Especially for a young, first-time mother, it was important to be with the people she knew and loved. But once again, Mary said yes. Not just because Rome ordered it, but also because—for some reason—God wanted it too.

So Mary embarked on her journey to Bethlehem. She and Joseph loaded the donkey with supplies and began their trek. Nine-months pregnant, she walked ninety miles. When she could no longer take another step, Joseph would place her on the back of the donkey. There were times when she longed to be at home, surrounded by her loved ones, for the journey was a difficult one. But there was also a strange sense of excitement. There were so many people on the roads because of the census. It reminded her of the time when she was little and the family traveled in a caravan to Jerusalem for Passover. Perhaps, as they passed through Jerusalem, she'd get to see the temple once again.

But with each exhausting and sometimes painful step, Mary sensed that out of this challenge would come something wonderful. She took in everything around her, soaking it up. Each encounter with another traveler, every new sight, became engraved in her memory.

It seems that when God calls us, we always end up on a road that leads us away from home. The road may not be easy, but it's never unbearable. If we are open, willing to connect with all that's around us, we see God in every chance meeting, in every shade tree, even in every stone that trips us up. Then, just when we think we can't take one more step, someone appears to lift us up and carry us until we can continue the journey. The road is to be embraced, not feared, because it leads us closer to Bethlehem, closer to God.

Joseph (Luke 2:1–7)

Good, dutiful, organized Joseph—how the decree must have upset him. You can almost imagine what he might have thought. "Curse those Romans! You can always count on them to make things harder. Now, of all times, to have to go to Bethlehem." Although Mary wasn't really due for another week or so, with a demanding journey, anything could happen. It would take five days to get to Bethlehem. What if Mary went into labor? What could he do? The men were always kept outside while the women helped deliver the babies. Following God this time meant going down a road he would prefer to avoid.

Joseph wasn't a romantic visionary like Mary. He was the practical one. He wouldn't dream of disobeying God, but you can bet he wouldn't leave Nazareth until everything was well planned. He studied the route, made provisions, and did his best to eliminate unwanted surprises. Builders hate surprises. You can imagine Joseph on the road, watchful, vigilant. Whenever possible he would caravan with other travelers so that Mary would be surrounded by women.

God calls the visionaries and the planners. God needs both. As you respond to God's call, you offer up every aspect of yourself. Wanting to do what's right and wanting to do it well aren't contrary to God's will. What does go against God's will is being so in control that you don't take into account that God may have other plans. Organizing things is okay; trying to control and organize God is not. It's not how you pack for the road that's important, it's being willing to take the journey and go wherever God leads you.

The Magi (Matthew 2:1–8)

The road for the magi was much longer. They came from the east—from Babylon, Media, and Persia. Separating them from Judea was the great Arabian Desert, so their trek began northward along the mighty Euphrates. The road was lush and beautiful and well traveled. It had been used for centuries, carrying merchants, armies, and captives. This was the road that Abraham traveled when God called him from Ur almost eighteen centuries earlier. Seven centuries before, the Babylonians took this route as they marched the captive Israelites into bondage. Now Babylonian magi were going to Jerusalem, not seeking captives, but seeking a king.

Then the caravan turned southward into the valleys of Mt. Hermon and through the mighty cedar forests of Lebanon. The long journey would have been exhausting and Damascus, the halfway point, provided a place to rest. Moving onward once again, the travelers came to the beautiful city of Caesarea Philippi, perched high on a terrace overlooking the entire Jordan valley. Each city was more beautiful than the last. Any of these cities would have been a suitable place for the birth of a king, but the magi kept going south toward Jerusalem. It must be Jerusalem, with its elegant palaces and breathtaking temple, where the king would be born. So these seekers of truth kept going, kept following the star, not knowing where it would lead them.

When we start out to follow that distant, beckoning voice, we don't know how long the journey will be or where it will end. We come to a place and say to ourselves, "This must be it. This must be what God intends." But it's not—it's just an oasis that provides a moment of rest and peace. Our journey has days of great beauty as well as days of dry and sandy deserts. We must remember that we are but passing through. Our destination, our hope, our calling is for one thing—to go to God and to present our offering: our hearts, our lives, our worship.

Obstacles

Mary (Luke 2:1–7)

The sun was beginning to set when they entered the city gates. The end of their journey was near. Relief poured over Mary like a gentle rain, washing away her fears. The bustle of the streets seemed to lift her spirits. Merchants were shouting in the marketplace. Wealthy and poor passed one another without much notice. There were Jews and Greeks and Egyptians and, yes, Romans. The Romans were mostly guards, always looking about, expecting the worst to happen.

Mary let herself indulge in the expectation of a long night's rest. She could almost feel the cool oil upon her face, cleansing away the dirt of the past five days. She longed to sleep on something softer than the ground. She'd been through so much, not just in the past five days, but in the past nine months. She'd endured the doubts of her family, the looks in the village, the anger and pain in Joseph's face. In all that time she never complained to God, not about what people thought or how hard the journey was. And now it was almost over, for in the last few miles she could tell that something was different. Her baby was coming, and he was coming soon.

The caravan stopped at an inn as dusk descended. "Sorry, no room," the innkeeper said. "If you ask around, you might find someone who will let you spend the night on their terrace." Mary's heart sank. She couldn't go on any longer. Just when she thought it was over, there was another obstacle in the path. The thought of going door-to-door asking for hospitality was more than she could bear. Tears began to roll down her face as she pleaded to God, "Father in heaven, can't it be easy, just this once?"

As the innkeeper started to shut the door, he noticed gentle sobs coming from behind Joseph. He looked over the traveler's shoulder and saw Mary—pregnant, dirty, and exhausted. "Wait," he said. "I have a cave back amongst the hills where I sometimes board my livestock. It's clean and dry and safe." The innkeeper took an oil lamp and escorted the young couple to the stable as the last rays of light escaped from behind the hills.

There are times in our journey when we think the end is in sight. The hard part is over and all we have to do is step across the finish line. Then, just as we're about to reach out and claim the prize, something happens that throws us off balance. This obstacle can seem like the hardest of all, because the end was so close. We cry out to God, "Just once, can't it be easy?"

The journey towards God can have moments of excitement, joy, and even rest, but it's unlikely that the journey will ever be easy. Easy is standing still. Easy is doing nothing. Moving forward always requires energy, determination, and letting go—and these are not easy things. When you begin to think it's easy, it's time to pay attention. Either you'll soon encounter a stone on your path or you're just standing still.

Joseph (Luke 2:1–7)

"No room!" Joseph could feel the blood rush to his face. His hand tightened on the donkey's rein. "What do you mean, no room?" Joseph asked, with as much restraint as he could muster. Good God! Enough is enough. He had dealt with the looks and innuendos of his village. He was forced to take Mary on this long journey because Caesar commanded it. He had to see his beloved Bethlehem, the City of David, occupied by Roman soldiers and census takers. And now, after he and Mary had finally arrived, he was told there was no place for them to stay. It seemed as if all of Joseph's strength and resolve gave way. Joseph was angry. In that moment, he cursed Caesar, the census takers, and the other travelers. He almost let out a curse at that blasted angel. He didn't, but he certainly let God know that he was upset. Why him? Why Mary? If this is the good news, then what's the bad?

When does your resolve to seek God's face begin to fade away? Think about those times when you were sure you were following

God's will. It may not have been easy, but you knew in your heart that it was what God wanted, and that was enough to keep you going. Then, all of a sudden, everything fell apart. Things didn't turn out as you'd planned or envisioned. Where, you wondered, was the fruit of your labor? You thought you were doing your part to build the kingdom of God, and now everything you'd worked for was in shambles. Perhaps you asked God, "What do you want from me, Lord?"

But did you ever wonder if perhaps the roadblocks we encounter in life aren't roadblocks at all? What if this is how God has planned it all along? We may see changes and twists in our plans as obstacles, but God may see them as midcourse corrections. It was God's plan from the beginning of time that Jesus would be born in a stable. Remember the story of another Joseph, the son of Jacob. He was sold into slavery by his brothers—certainly a calamity, but it got him to Egypt, where he learned to be a manager in Potiphar's household. Things were going well once again until Potiphar's wife tried to seduce him and had him thrown in jail. Joseph could have called out to God, "Why have you abandoned me?" But he didn't—because in time, circumstances led him to Pharaoh. And in good time, as Pharaoh's right-hand man, he saved Egypt and his own family from starvation. So much for obstacles. At the end of the story, Joseph says to his brothers, "Even though you intended to do harm to me, God intended it for good."

If you encounter obstacles on your journey, don't assume they're roadblocks. They may be just directional arrows pointing you to God's true path.

The Magi (Matthew 2:1–8)

The magi finally reached Jerusalem. They had overcome many obstacles already, but this last one was of a different sort. They'd come here in search of a king, yet there was nothing to indicate that a king had been born—no celebrations, no decrees, no flurry of activity around the palace. They asked around the city, but no one knew anything of a child born king of the Jews. If they were looking for a newborn king, wasn't it reasonable to first go to the palace of the current king? Obviously not. They apparently knew enough about Herod not to trust him—his reputation for killing off heirs to the throne was well known. It seemed unlikely to the magi that the true king would be born into the household of Herod.

Deserts, mountains, heat, long distances—none of these things had stopped them. They'd made it all this way in search of the truth only to find a dead end. They were frustrated—and puzzled. They were the only ones even looking for this special king. They were longing to find him so they could give him honor and worship. They had gifts to present that were useless unless they could get them to this newborn babe. Didn't anyone know or care what had happened? Where were the priests, the prophets, and the holy men? Here, in the country of the Jews, the magi were searching for the king of the Jews—so why were they the only ones looking? And why was everyone else unaware that something wonderful had happened in their midst?

The religious leaders were no help. But help would come, from a rather unexpected source. One night the magi received a sealed message from King Herod summoning them to the palace. An exchange of information took place. They told him the date the star first appeared, and he told them in which city they could find the babe. As they turned to leave, Herod called out to them, "Oh, and on your way back, please stop and tell me where you found this king so that I may go and worship him, too." The obstacle had been removed—and by Herod, of all people.

As you continue on your pilgrimage to Christ, you'll also encounter many obstacles. One of the hardest is finding out that God's people can be obstacles themselves. Coming from outside Israel, the magi could see the star. They were clear and focused in their search. But the people of Jerusalem were oblivious. The story of the true king of the Jews, the Messiah, had been around for a very long time. For centuries, the prophets had reminded the people about the Messiah's coming. But on the night the magi arrived in Jerusalem, there hadn't been a prophet for four hundred years. The Messiah had become irrelevant to most people. They were so busy with their lives and with their religious rituals that they'd stopped looking for the king.

Think of a time when you were hungry to know more about God. Who did you ask for guidance? Did you ever find that the people you expected to help you, couldn't? How did that make you feel? Did it make you feel like you were on your own? Did it make you sad or even angry? Think about why the religious establishment couldn't help you. Perhaps the Church was so busy doing things that it didn't leave room for simply knowing God. Maybe some people wanted to help you but they just didn't know how.

When we're hungry for God, God sees to it that we get what we need. God's hands are not tied by the sinful brokenness of humanity. An individual may let you down. A church or an organization may let you down. But this doesn't mean that God will let you down. God will use anything and anyone to show us the way.

Sometimes God comes to us in ways unexpected. We can't use the Church as an excuse for not growing. Our spiritual growth is not dependent on the quality of the preacher, the depth of the Sunday school curriculum, or the number of members in the choir. God can still speak to you through meager means. We also can't let failed expectations deter us from our call. Even things that seem like insurmountable barriers—the Israelite's lack of understanding, their malaise, and their sin—aren't obstacles to God after all. At times, the people of God may let you down. God never will.

ENCOUNTERING GOD

Mary (Luke 2:6–19)

We know nothing of what happened that night in the stable. There is nothing to indicate, however, that Mary was any different from any other woman who has given birth throughout the centuries. This was no immaculate delivery; it was very real and very natural. Mary's encounter with the holy that night involved tears of joy, cries of pain, and hours of great effort. Only a woman who has given birth knows what she felt that night.

Some legends say that the innkeeper's wife came out to act as midwife. Surely Joseph was there to help in whatever way he could. No matter who was there, this was Mary's time. Others could have comforted her, given her advice, or wiped her brow, but the work was Mary's alone. The coming of God into her life at that moment was very intense and very private.

Then a quiet stillness fell on the stable. Mary cradled her newborn child close to her breast. So much had led to this moment and now all the waiting was over. As she gazed on the face of her tiny son, everything that came before faded. There was no thought of the angel or of the strange pronouncement of her cousin Elizabeth. It was just a mother and her baby.

But something happened that brought it all back. Someone was coming. Mary and Joseph heard voices and commotion coming toward the stable. They didn't know how many were coming, but they knew it was more than one or two. Was it highwaymen, or perhaps Roman soldiers? Mary held her newborn tightly and moved back out of the light as Joseph stepped forward and called out to the men now standing at the opening of the cave. "Who are you and what do you want?" They replied, "We are shepherds from the hills who have come to see the baby. We were told of his birth by God's messengers." Mary turned toward the light and bid them to come in.

As they huddled around the mother and child, the shepherds told Mary and Joseph all that had happened that night. They told of the first angel, then of the multitude of angels that followed. They told of how the glory of heaven appeared. Then they spoke of the most exciting thing of all, the words that the angels had proclaimed: "For this night the Messiah is born, and he can be found in Bethlehem."

The Messiah. The long-awaited deliverer of Israel had come and it was her son. All the pieces started to make sense, started to fit together. The angel, the pronouncements, all that had happened these past nine months were now clear. This child is the Messiah. Mary pondered these words and kept them in her heart. She understood.

When we set out to follow God, we have no idea what will happen. We say, "Sure, God, whatever you want." We, in our childlike faith, have no clue what it means to say yes to God, but still we trust God to take our hand and lead us on the journey. Obstacles come, and so do moments of fear and doubt. "Is this a safe God?" we may wonder. "Did God lead me out here and abandon me?" There are times when we want to quit and run away, and sometimes we do. But when we stay on the path we come to this moment: we come to the presence of God.

The journey isn't always easy and its culmination can be like giving birth—full of pain and joy, tears and laughter. But once we gaze on the Son, the pieces start to fit. What puzzled us before begins to make sense. We see with new eyes. We begin to understand. We don't have it all figured out because this isn't really the end. It's just the beginning. Encountering the holy, we need to be still and ponder what it means, like Mary did that night, and hold that knowledge in our hearts for all time.

Joseph (Luke 2:6–19)

Joseph had the hands of a carpenter, broad and rough. In those strong but gentle hands he held the newborn babe. "So tiny, so helpless," he thought. His heart swelled with a love he'd never known.

Of course he loved Mary. He loved his parents and his brothers and sisters, too. But this was different. This was a protective, fearsome type of love. When the shepherds came, Joseph realized that he would have done anything to protect the child. Joseph was resolute that no harm would ever come to this child. As long as he lived, he would make sure of that.

But for now, his alarm was unfounded. The shepherds brought good news. This child was God's own son, the Messiah. God's son! Even though he had never been with Mary, he had never thought of this child as any other but his own. Joseph didn't know how Mary came to be with child; he just believed God's words that she was pregnant by the Holy Spirit. It didn't matter to Joseph how God performed the miracle—this was still his child. He was Mary's husband and this child was as much a gift to him as it was to Mary.

There are times that we come to the stable with rough, unworthy hands. Without shame or fear of rebuke, we draw close to God and hold tight. We breathe in God's fragrance and feel God's tender caress. God is totally other, yet dwells in us as we dwell in God. Awesome and above being possessed by mere mortals, this mighty God calls us friend and beloved child. God's fearsome love for us led to the cross where Jesus died for us. Once we have truly known God, that same fearsome love compels us to lay our life on the line, pick up our cross, and follow.

The Magi (Matthew 2:9–11)

At long last, their quest—begun two years earlier when they first spied the star in the western sky—was over. The planning, the preparation, the trek itself took a greater toll than they expected. The journey would have been hard even for young men, and their bodies constantly reminded them that they were not as young as they used to be.

When they reached the humble abode where Joseph and Mary stayed, the magi were filled with joy—the joy of realizing their dream, of meeting this special babe, and of finally bringing this long, arduous pilgrimage to an end. They came to the house looking much like other travelers. They dressed as other travelers, for comfort and practicality. The last thing they wanted was to draw attention to themselves. They carried precious cargo for this newborn king and didn't want to attract the attention of the bandits who lurked along the roads.

When the magi arrived and asked if they could see the child, Joseph and Mary agreed to let them in. "Kindly old gentlemen," they thought. The magi told of the star and of their mission to pay homage to this baby. It wasn't until they opened several small chests to reveal gifts of gold, frankincense, and myrrh that Mary and Joseph realized that there was more to these gentlemen than met the eye.

As for the magi, they were struck with a sense of awe they'd never before experienced. They'd served in the courts of rich and powerful kings and studied the heavens and all its wonders. But this helpless infant took their breath away. For a fleeting moment, they felt shame over the gifts they had brought. Next to this child, this king, the gifts seemed so unworthy.

If you've been on life's journey for a long time and have seen much, you might understand how the magi felt. You're no longer innocent or naive. You may have done well in life. When you come to church, you bring your offerings—gifts of time, talent, and treasure. You may even have a sense of pride about your spiritual journey or in the value of your gifts. But when you encounter Christ—really encounter him—things take on a different perspective. You know what greatness is, and you know that it has nothing to do with whom you work for or how much you earn—or even with how much you give. Greatness is the extravagant love of God hanging on the cross for the sins of the whole world.

Go Forth!

Mary (Luke 2:21–35)

Mary's time of purification was over. She had spent thirty-three days set apart from the rest of the world with only Joseph and Jesus by her side, completely sheltered from all of life's cares and worries. But now, she and Joseph had to go to Jerusalem, to the temple, to offer sacrifice for their firstborn son. Mary stepped out of the safety of her room and into a world that would never be the same again.

The temple was bustling and crowded as always. Joseph wanted to purchase a lamb for the sacrifice, but that was too expensive. "We'll need our money for other things," is all he said. So they bought two pigeons, as the law required. Joseph, holding tightly to the sacrifice, led Mary through the courtyard and into the temple. As they made their way through the women's court to the Beautiful Gate, Mary noticed an elderly man coming toward them. He seemed so ancient that Mary wondered how he could even get around, yet with each step he moved faster and faster until he was almost running. Wide-eyed and out of breath, the old man came up to Mary and asked if he could hold the baby, just for a moment. Joseph didn't think it was a good idea, but Mary knew it was safe. Joyfully the old man exclaimed:

> Lord, you now have set your servant free
> to go in peace as you have promised;
> For these eyes of mine have seen the Savior,
> whom you have prepared for all the world to see:
> A Light to enlighten the nations,
> and the glory of your people Israel. (BCP, 93)

Mary was amazed by what the old man was saying, but that amazement soon turned to heaviness and fear. The old man turned directly to Mary and spoke ever so softly: "This child is destined for the falling and the rising of many in Israel, and to be a sign that will be opposed so that the inner thoughts of many will be revealed, and a sword will pierce your own soul too."

Mary's first call was to come and be filled with the presence of God. Her second call was to give it all back. Jesus was not hers to hold onto. As much as Jesus would grow to love her and Joseph, he would never really be fully theirs. The angels, the proclamations, the prophecies—all took on a new perspective for Mary. The sword the old man talked about wasn't something that would happen someday. It happened at that moment. Mary's heart was pierced then and there and she would carry the wound the rest of her life.

What have you sacrificed for God? What beautiful gift did God give you that you had to sacrifice on the altar? As servants of God, there are times when we expect—or at least hope—that things will go a certain way. We do our part, walk in God's ways, and in return expect to reap the benefits. We may not demand it, it's just one of the nice blessings we get for being God's servants. But what if the blessings don't come? What if all we have at the end of the day is the knowledge that we were good and faithful servants? Is this enough? Can we walk around with a wounded heart and still love God? Mary did.

Joseph (Matthew 2:13–15)

"Maybe now we can get back to normal," thought Joseph—no more men from strange foreign lands, no more smelly shepherds, and especially no more angelic visitors! Joseph started to arrange for their return home to Nazareth. Then, once again while he slept, God's messenger came to him, "Flee, Joseph! Get up now and make your way to Egypt." Herod knew about Jesus' birth and was determined to kill him. Herod would do anything to stay in power—anything.

Joseph awoke and gathered as many belongings as the donkey could carry. Once everything was ready, he tenderly bent down and woke Mary. "Come, Mary," he said, "we must take our child and flee this country. The Lord's angel came to me in a dream and told us to leave for Egypt this very night." Mary was neither frightened nor reluctant. She trusted in God to watch over them. She also trusted Joseph.

In this predawn escape, Joseph led his family away from everything familiar. They were going to a foreign country, and all they could take was what they could carry. Unlike the trip to Bethlehem, this time they'd be traveling alone along an unfamiliar road. Joseph couldn't help but wonder what would become of them. What if they got to Egypt and the Lord told them to go even farther? How would he support his family? How could he find work in Egypt? He didn't even speak the language! That night, the burden in Joseph's heart was much heavier than the burden the donkey bore. But Joseph kept going. He was obedient to God. It didn't matter what he left behind. The only things that mattered were Mary and Jesus, and the knowledge that God was leading the way. No matter how uncertain or unfamiliar the future seemed that night, Joseph knew that he and Mary were not alone.

Once you've had an experience of God, as Joseph did, you can't simply go back to where you were. Life doesn't go on as if nothing had happened. The world may look the same and you may even act the same, but you're not the same. You've changed, and because of that everything else has changed too. Your old lifestyle, your old pleasures, even your old friends seem somehow different. At first it can be frightening and strange, but with each new step you'll feel the presence of God leading you forward. New lands, new people, and new adventures await. Don't look back and cry over what you left. Look ahead and smile over what you'll surely find.

The Magi (Matthew 2:12)

The years of study, the anticipation, the long journey—and now the quest had come to an end. The magi had finally seen the king spoken of in the prophecies. So now what? Where would their studies lead them next? They were men of science; they were explorers and men of wisdom. They lived to ask questions and to seek the truth. Now that they'd found this child-king, surely God had other mysteries to show them.

They talked about the future long into the night. They knew they needed to return home and tell others about this baby. They longed to pore over their books and maps to see what God would show them next. The magi knew that the end of a quest isn't the end of the story—it's the beginning of a new one. They resolved to get some rest and return home the next day.

But they didn't have to wait until they returned home for God to show them what to do. Their sleep was disturbed by dreams—dreams of pain, anguish, and death. They heard the mournful wailing of countless women. In the midst of all the turmoil stood Herod, his hands and his kingly robes covered in blood. Herod looked at the magi and said, "Tell me where he is, so that I may worship him also."

The magi awoke and ran out of their tents, half-expecting to see soldiers brandishing swords. But the night was dark and still. As they stood facing one another in the darkness, they knew what this dream meant. It was a warning.

By the time the sun was up, the magi were ready to depart. First, they confided the warning to Joseph, who had already had a dream of his own. Then they began their journey home, this time avoiding Jerusalem. They'd have to find another way. Perhaps they could go south into Arabia, to the trade city of Epah and then north across the desert to Babylon. There'd be no beautiful Euphrates and glistening cities this trip, just desert and the occasional oasis. They returned home, but it wasn't the journey they had expected.

Scripture is the story of a journey. Everyone we encounter when we read the Bible is on a journey. God calls us either to "come" and join him or to "go forth" into the world. Most of the heroes in Scripture venture off into new and unknown places without the benefit of a roadmap—and sometimes without even a destination. And those few who do go home again never go back the way they came. They find a new way home and a deeper transformation. The stories in the Bible show us that we can return to our old location, but we go back as different people. Our eyes have been opened to new sights. We see things with a whole new sense of purpose and being. Transformed by our journey, we begin to see as God sees.

The Second Movement:
Walking in the Light

Epiphany

STEPPING OUT

Our walk to Bethlehem is over, but our true journey is about to
begin. The Christ Child no longer lies in a manger in a land far away.
He is playing with the other children down the street. He is losing at
checkers at the senior center. He is laughing and singing in the rush of
a new love. He is weeping with those who are suffering. He is in the
face of your spouse, your child, your parent, and the stranger who
passes you on the street. Listen for God's voice in your dreams, in the
words of crazy old men and women, and in the depths of his holy
Word. Listen, for God is calling you to draw close. Go and see. Go and
hear. The King is waiting for you.

Simeon (Luke 2:21–35, Revised Common Lectionary 4C)

So long. It had been so long. Simeon had waited a lifetime to
behold God's anointed. But what was that wait compared to the wait
Israel had had to endure? It had been more than four hundred years
since the last prophet had walked among them. But God's promise
was there and it wouldn't go away.

LORD, how long will you forget me? Forever?
How long will you look the other way?
How long must I struggle with anguish in my soul,
With sorrow in my heart every day?
(Psalm 13:1–2, New Living Translation)

Every morning Simeon rose from his bed and offered his morning
prayer. "Is this the day?" he would ask. "Is this the day I will behold
the Messiah?" The same prayer, day after day, year after year, God
remained silent. The deafening silence of God.

On the best of days, Simeon would recall the Spirit's presence
and revel in the awesome knowledge that he would live to see the
Messiah, God's anointed!

On the worst of days, he would question whether he'd ever
heard God's voice at all. Was it just a dream, the wishful imaginings
of a lonely heart? Did his longing for God's comfort fill his mind
with selfish desires? But desire God he did. This was the desire that
kept him going even when it looked as if the promise would never
come true.

Then, after years of waiting, in the very twilight of Simeon's life,
God answered. "Today, Simeon. Today you will see my son." How the
old man's heart must have pounded! Moving as fast as his ancient legs
could carry him, Simeon began his journey to Christ. How would he
know the Messiah? The crowd was large. As he made his way through
the crowd, images passed in his mind. Seeing a tall, handsome man,
he would wonder, "Is that he? Will God's anointed know me? Will he
come up to me or must I find him in the throng?" Excitement, worry,
anticipation, fear—all these emotions flooded Simeon as he stood
before the great gate of the temple. God's temple. God's son. How
would he know? How could he tell after all these years?

Out of the corner of his eye, Simeon glimpsed a young couple
making their way to the moneychangers. The man was rough and
strong. The woman looked almost regal as she carried a tiny child.

Regal looking yet poor, they seemed, for they were able to afford only two small pigeons. As Simeon gazed on them, the Spirit of God moved in him. "There, Simeon; there is the one." "That man?" he wondered aloud. "No. The babe. He is the consolation of Israel." All the aches and pains of old age, all the layers of discouragement and doubt vanished as Simeon quickly made his way to the young couple. Smiling at the woman, he asked if he could hold the child. As their eyes met, it became clear that this was all part of God's plan. Holding the tiny child in his arms, he spoke: "Lord, now I can die in peace! As you promised me, I have seen the Savior you have given to all people. He is a light to reveal God to the nations, and he is the glory of your people Israel!" (NLT).

How many times have we prayed, like Simeon, to a God who doesn't seem to answer—or even to care? Our tears and our blood become mingled as we cry out to God: "How long, God? How long will you let me suffer?" There are days when we want to quit. There are days when it's all we can do to get out of bed. Even on those days, the promise endures.

God's promise is that our consolation is at hand. We don't know when or how God's healing touch will come to us. Simeon didn't know—he just waited and prayed. Then the urging came. Simeon listened and followed.

Listen to the urgings of God. Anticipate God's light. Listen for answers you don't expect and be open to solutions you don't see coming.

Simeon's task was done. The promise had been fulfilled and the old man could return home. As he turned from the temple and began heading back, Simeon walked in the shalom of God, in the completeness of God's grace and love. He had seen and touched the anointed one. His answered prayers had become flesh. His pain and heartache—and the pain of all Israel—could now be healed. After all those long years of waiting, the answer was more than he could have imagined.

Now he could die with no regrets or remorse, because his life's plan has been completed. Was that all there was left to do—just go home and die? Was his journey home his last journey? Did it lead to death? We don't know. We know nothing else about Simeon. We don't know if God made other promises or had other plans for him. But we do know that that for Simeon—and for us—all our journeys lead to death. That is our lot. But the God of creation never expects us to just lie down and wait for it. Instead, God calls us to always and everywhere be co-creators in building the kingdom. God didn't promise Simeon that he would die when the Messiah came. God promised Simeon that he wouldn't die before that day.

Reflect on the times you've accomplished a great goal or achieved an exhilarating success. What feelings did you have after the exultation subsided? Perhaps you were a little depressed. Not having a dream can leave a big void—without vision, Scripture tells us, the people perish. Achieving a dream or a goal can leave you feeling lost, lacking vision or direction. Celebrate your accomplishment, but not for too long. Listen for what God has in store for you now. Our calling never comes to an end. When one task is completed, God has already prepared another for us. Simeon's journey didn't end. It just took a different turn.

Nathanael (John 1:43–52, Epiphany 2C)

It was a perfect day. The afternoon sun was casting a warm glow over the Sea of Galilee. Nathanael's work for the day was done, and he rested under the cool shade of the fig tree as he studied the Torah, looking and praying for the deliverance of Israel. He'd made friends with other young men who were also eagerly awaiting the Messiah. With Peter, Andrew, and Philip, he'd gone out to hear John preach and been baptized by him. The Messiah was coming soon.

He knew it. John was the sign. So he sat under the fig tree—the best place, the rabbis said, to study Torah—and pleaded with God to send the Messiah.

Full of hope and anticipation, Nathanael started back to the place he was spending the night when Philip ran up the path. Even his step indicated there was news. Excitedly, Nathanael greeted his friend, "Philip, what is it? Why the excitement?"

"We've found him, Nathanael! We've found the one Moses and the prophets wrote about. He's Jesus of Nazareth, son of Joseph."

A little laugh escaped from the back of Nathanael's throat. "Nazareth?" he demanded. "Can anything good come out of Nazareth?" Nathanael had grown up in Cana, just nine miles north of Nazareth, and knew that little village well. Today, a few millennia later, we could describe the two towns as acting like high school rivals. "Can anything good come out of Nazareth?" he wondered again, and not just because he knew Nazareth. He also knew Scripture. A king from the line of David wouldn't come from Nazareth!

But Philip insisted. "Just come and see, Nathanael. That's all I'm asking of you. Just come and see." So reluctantly, out of trust in his friend and out of curiosity, he went to meet the man Philip said was the one.

Nathanael got there in no time, and when he did, Jesus startled him profoundly. He looked at Nathanael before they'd even been introduced and said: "Behold, an Israelite in whom there is no guile."

Nathanael was taken aback. It wasn't just one compliment he received from Jesus but two. This Jesus didn't address him as Jew, but with the more respectful title of Israelite. And on top of that, he proclaimed him a man of innocence and integrity. Anxiously, Nathanael murmured, "How do you know me?"

The answer was more startling still. "Before Philip found you," Jesus replied, "I saw you under the fig tree." No one knew what Nathanael had been doing there except God alone, yet this Jesus of

Nazareth saw and knew what was in his heart. Philip had to be right. This was the one. Praise be to God—all his hopes and dreams were coming true, just as he knew they would.

We study and we pray and we trust in God. Then it happens— our prayers are answered. But wait. It's not exactly as we thought it would be. According to what we know and understand, things should look different. The answer should come wrapped in a different package or with more pomp and circumstance. Surely something so simple, so common, so close, can't be the answer from God. But it is. All we have to do is continue to trust and then—like Nathanael—go and see. It's in the seeing that God overcomes our objections. Don't let knowledge get in the way, because knowledge is only the guide to Christ and not the relationship itself. Sit, study, pray. Then put your books away, get up, and go and see.

Nathanael found what he was looking for not in some far-off city or remote mountaintop, but practically in his back yard. He found the Messiah among his own friends, in his own region. Walking a familiar road, he came across a companion who simply said, "Come and see." Getting past his doubts and expectations, Nathanael went and saw and was rewarded with a promise from God's chosen one. Nathanael was told that, like Jacob, he'd see the heavens open and the angels of God ascending and descending upon the Son of Man.

What an answer to prayer! What a spectacular vision! And it all happened just a few miles from home. Then it got even better, because Jesus invited Nathanael to follow him. And follow him he did, right back to his hometown of Cana. The answer to all of Israel's prayers was coming home with Nathanael.

Questions flooded Nathanael's mind. Would his neighbors and relatives recognize the Messiah as he had? How would they receive Jesus? How would they receive Nathanael himself—could they tell just by looking at him that something amazing had happened? Each step closer to Cana made Nathanael's heart beat even harder. Perspiration was pouring from his forehead and his hands, not from strenuous walking but from all the activity going on in his mind. "I've found him," he thought to himself, "and I'm bringing him home."

As Jesus and his new disciples came into the town, it was bustling with excitement. And everyone's face was flushed with revelry. But the crowd, Nathanael realized, wasn't focused on Nathanael and this stranger from Nazareth. In fact, nobody seemed to notice them at all.

"Wait a minute," he wanted to yell to the noisy crowd, "I've found him! I've brought home the chosen one of God." But the villagers thronged past them as if they didn't even exist. Something more important than the salvation of Israel was going on. There was a wedding.

Christ told us that the kingdom of God is at hand—as if we could reach out and literally touch it. Yet we go through our lives either looking for it in some far-off place or ignoring it altogether in the busy-ness of our lives. Nathanael couldn't open his eyes to see that God's promise could come from something so common as the neighboring village. Once his eyes were opened, however, he didn't understand how everyone else could be so blind.

We go on retreats, conferences, and workshops hoping to find the kingdom of God in a set-apart place. Perhaps if we just opened our eyes and ears as we walk our neighborhoods, parks, and malls, we'd see the light right in front of us.

But when we do see the light—when our prayers for a relationship with God are answered—we can't expect others to see the same thing. Remember that they are as blind to God's reality as we once were. Their eyes will never be opened if all we convey is frustration, disappointment, anger, or impatience. Remember that Nathanael overcame his objections to Christ because his friend Philip invited rather than pushed. Remember what it's like to be Nathanael, and remember the Nathanael in others. Don't push. Just lovingly extend your hand and say, "Come and see."

The Leper (Mark 1:40–45, Epiphany 6B)

He was totally forgotten. He existed only in the shadows. The sun was his enemy—just a few moments of exposure caused his skin to suffer excruciating pain. Even so, the physical pain of his flesh was less than the pain in his soul, because what he missed the most was the touch of another human being. He'd been isolated in the darkness for so long that he almost forgot what it felt like to be held, to be caressed. There were no hands to comfort him during the long, lonely nights. There were no lips to kiss away his tears. Each day he disappeared more and more into the shadows.

But even in the shadows, one hears things. Whispers travel. One such whisper spoke of a miracle man from Galilee—a rabbi named Jesus who was healing people. Talk was that in Capernaum the crowd was so large that Jesus had to escape into the wilderness. Jesus could heal the sick. He could cast out demons. Could he do the impossible? Could this Jesus heal someone with leprosy? Could he be as great as the prophet Elisha?

Here in the shadows, this man—this leper—knew that Jesus was traveling throughout the towns of Galilee. The leper had to find Jesus. He had to know for himself. But that meant stepping out of the shadows and back into the light. He had to risk the pain—not only the pain of the sun and the road, but the pain of rejection. Lepers who went out among the healthy would be cursed and vilified, perhaps even stoned. The whispers said Jesus was merciful, but even Jesus could turn him away. What was there to lose at this point? Nothing. He was already a man who didn't exist. He went.

The road was hard on his feet. It had been a long time since he had walked any distance. His body and face were covered with a woolen blanket to block the rays of the sun. The heat and the coarseness of the blanket against his skin were almost as unbearable as the sun itself. Yet he moved on, cautiously hopeful.

It took several days, but he found him. The leper could hear them talking and laughing even before he saw Jesus walking along the road with his disciples. Then he heard the familiar warning: "Leper!" This was his cue to turn aside and keep his distance from the healthy people. But not today. Instead, he took a few more steps toward Jesus and then dropped to his knees. He was terrified but his heart was sure that this Jesus could be God's chosen one. He lifted his hands as beggars do. "Lord, if you want to, you can make me well again."

Jesus looked down on the leper and smiled. Love emanated from every part of him as he reached down and touched the quivering being kneeling before him. A simple touch, so long denied, and two words—"Be healed"—were all it took. A touch from Jesus and everything changed! The leper felt a gentle warmth, not like the intense heat of the sun. He was aware of light everywhere, but it wasn't blinding or harsh. Basking in this loving light, the leper let the cloth fall from his body, kneeling for what felt like an eternity. Then he looked down at his hands. They were clean! No lesions! He stood up. His legs and his feet were strong. The sun didn't burn. He was healed! Jesus had healed him.

We all spend time in the shadows. Perhaps we live there for a few days or months. Perhaps it becomes a more permanent home as we slowly become disconnected from others. When we lose our connectedness, we lose our identities and become invisible to the rest of the world. There seems to be no one to hold our hands or kiss away our tears. Pain eats away at our souls just as much as leprosy eats away at the flesh. It can be so tempting to lie down and let the shadows enfold us.

But there is hope. There is healing. There is Jesus. Emerging from the shadows and turning to Christ can be painful. The journey requires effort as we go beyond our comfort zones. We may have to exchange our old familiar pain for new, unknown pain. We may have to step forward and face the harshness that the world sometimes provides. But that is where we find God. It is our faith that brings us to God. It is faith that says light is stronger than darkness, that hope is stronger than despair, that love is stronger than hate.

Begin your journey out of the shadows. Turn to the light of Christ with bold determination. Jesus desires that you be whole. Seek him. Ask him. He will answer your prayers.

Everything changed! In an instant, the leper's world had been turned upside down. He was a new creation—free of the disease, the pain, the fear, the shame. His newfound voice wanted to shout to the entire world, "I've been healed!"

Then Jesus spoke once again. "Go, show yourself to the priest, and offer for your cleansing what Moses commanded," he said. Of course, he needed a clean bill of health—and only the priests could officially take care of that. But then Jesus gave him very strange instructions. "Don't talk to anyone along the way," he warned. "Go straight there and take the offering required for those who have been healed of leprosy. That will be the proof of your healing."

With his mind awhirl, the leper went looking for the items he needed—two wild game birds, some cedar wood, a scarlet cloth, and a hyssop branch for the purification ceremony. And that would be just the beginning. Next would come the cleansing of his clothes, the shaving of all his hair, and the ritual cleansing of his body. Even then, he wouldn't be able to return to the community. He'd still have to live apart for seven days and be shaved and washed again. Finally, on the eighth and last day would come the sacrifice of thanksgiving—two male lambs and one female year-old lamb, five quarts of flour, and a jar of olive oil.

Jesus wanted him to wait eight days before he told of the miracle. "Why?" he thought. This is such wonderful news. It should be told now. How could he keep such a thing quiet? He ran and stumbled as he went, seeking the necessary items. The crowds looked at him strangely. He acted almost as if he were mad. The man couldn't hold back any longer. He began to blurt out what had happened to him. He spoke of his leprosy. He told of the rabbi Jesus. He described the rabbi's touch and how it felt. He reveled in sharing the coming of the warmth and light. It was all too wonderful to keep inside. It was a tale he had to tell.

We don't know what became of the man who was a leper. We do know that the excitement he created made Jesus even more of a celebrity—he couldn't walk into any town without the crowds overwhelming him and preventing him from doing his work. Jesus had to find other ways to reach the people. It may not have really mattered all that much in the long run, but the man's disobedience to Christ did change things. We'll never know what might have happened if the leper had just obeyed.

Good news is meant to be shared. God wants us to be witnesses to the ends of the earth. But how? The best way is with our lives. In the words attributed to St. Francis of Assisi, we're called to "preach the Gospel at all times, and if necessary, use words."

The more we talk about our experience, the more the focus can shift from God's act to ours. It becomes "my story" and not the story of God in my life. If God has changed you, don't be overly concerned with telling everybody. Live the new life you've been given. Living as a new creation gets people's attention. "Isn't that so-and-so?" they'll wonder. "What a change! I'd sure like to know how *that* happened."

The greatest evangelistic tool isn't a program or a technique. It's living a life that is changed.

The Paralytic (Mark 2:1–12, Epiphany 7B)

He should have been bitter. After the accident left his legs broken and paralyzed, his livelihood was destined to be begging for scraps along the streets of Capernaum. Society labeled him an outcast. Obviously, people thought, his accident was punishment for some horrible sin he had committed. He could no longer go to temple or synagogue. His infirmity had made him unclean.

But it wasn't like that. He wasn't bitter. He had friends—the kind of friends who don't leave you when things get tough. They were the kind of friends who stayed by him, who cared for him, who made sure he had what was needed. They were the kind of friends who told him about Jesus the miracle worker.

Who in Capernaum didn't know about this young rabbi and his disciples? People flocked to him to be cured of their illnesses until he abruptly left town. Talk was that he couldn't take the crowds any longer, and many wondered if he'd run out of miracles. But rumors kept finding their way back to Capernaum. Jesus was healing all throughout Galilee—he'd even made a leper clean! And now the talk was that he was back in town. Jesus had returned and this man's friends were going to make sure that this time their friend would be one of those healed.

The four friends came and lifted the paralyzed man with his mat. They carried him through the city streets to the home of Jesus' disciple, Simon Peter. But turning the corner onto Peter's street, their hearts fell. The crowd was large and noisy, and so many people were trying to push into the doorway that there was no way to get in. But nothing was going to stop these stalwart friends from completing their mission. They had to bring their companion to Jesus, no matter what it took.

They looked around for another way into the house, but there was none. The houses were small and built closely together, with barely enough room to walk between them. They were so close that a person could step from one roof to another. They thought for a moment. If they could only get their friend up on a roof, they could walk above the crowd and make their way to Peter's house.

They found a house nearby with its ladder to the roof already in place. It wasn't easy, but they lifted their friend up the ladder and onto the rooftop, then carried him across to the next house. First, two of the friends jumped across. With two on one roof and two on another, they strained and pulled the man's mat until he had crossed over the chasm. They did it once, twice, and finally reached the house in which Jesus was teaching. "Now how do we get him inside?" they asked themselves.

Looking over the edge, they couldn't find any way into the house. But they'd come this far, so this was no time for timidity. They began to chip away at the roof's clay surface until they came to the twigs and branches that made up the middle layer. Using their bare hands, they tore away the dried leaves to find the saplings that formed the roof frame. Everyone in the house knew what was happening by the time they broke through the final layer. Through the gaping hole, the four friends slowly lowered the paralyzed man down into the room below, right in front of Jesus himself. Once he was safely on the ground, the friends jumped inside.

They were ready for anything. Certainly the people in the house would be upset, but they had to explain before an angry crowd threw them out. They stood up, ready to defend themselves, but were astonished to see Jesus laughing. The crowd stood by in stunned silence, but Jesus was obviously delighted by the whole scene.

"Surely," Jesus said to the paralyzed man, "you are blessed to have such friends. You are no longer unclean, for your sins have been forgiven!" Instantaneously, the paralyzed man felt whole once again. He couldn't describe this strange sensation, for it came from deep within him.

The crowd murmured. Jesus turned to them and said, "Why do you think it is blasphemy to forgive sins? Is it easier to say to the paralyzed man, 'Your sins are forgiven,' or 'Get up and walk'?" Jesus looked back at the paralyzed man and spoke. "I will prove that I, the

Son of Man, have the power to forgive sins," he said. "Stand up, take up your mat, and go home because you are healed."

How many times in life have our friends and loved ones carried us to Christ? Maybe they've literally carried us to church by driving when we couldn't, or maybe they brought Christ to us in the sacrament. How many times have they figuratively carried us to Christ in their prayers during the seasons in our spiritual journey when we could no longer take another step and we lay alongside the road ready to give up and let the journey continue without us?

Blessed are those who have friends who won't let them give up. Blessed are those whose friends care enough to go the distance, to hang in there when everyone else says enough. When our faith is weak, it's enough to have friends whose faith is strong. We can truly find healing and light in the faith of those who care enough to bring us before God.

He came to Christ born on the shoulders of his faithful friends. He left jumping and praising God on his own two feet. Without the faith of his friends, there would have been no healing. This man owed his health, his salvation—everything—to those four friends. Yet it wasn't the friends who had healed him. It was Jesus.

Scripture tells us that they all praised God for what had happened. How easy it would have been for the paralyzed man to praise his friends rather than God. We've seen it happen that way. A person comes to Christ through the teaching of a particular pastor or teacher or encounters God in a small group. As time passes, the teacher or group takes on more and more power and authority, until the person's gratitude is no longer extended to God but to the tools God used. Subtly and without knowing it, the journey no longer leads to Christ but to idolatry.

Another danger is never growing a faith of your own. It's so easy to rely on the faith of others. But although the faith of our loved ones is important, it's not meant as a substitute for growing in grace ourselves. The faith of others brought the paralytic to Christ, but his own faith sent him out into the world. As you walk this meditation, think of those people who have carried you when your body was weak or your faith was lacking. See them walking beside you as they bring you face-to-face with Jesus. As you stand before Jesus, imagine your friend smiling at you and saying: "Now it's your turn. It's time to stand on your own two feet before God."

Stand before Jesus and let him bless you. Hear the words of healing he has for you. Take them in, feel his love and forgiveness. When the time is right, begin your journey once again. But this time, you're by yourself. You don't need your friend to carry you. You find that you can walk on your own because you've been changed. Jesus has healed you.

As you continue your spiritual journey, there will again be times when you need to be carried. There will also times when you'll be called on to carry someone else. We're all on this journey together, and we all need one another from time to time. It's just part of being on the road.

The Transfiguration (Matthew 17:1–9, Last Sunday of Epiphany)

Jesus said, "Come with me. There is something I must do." So they went—Peter, James, and John. Leaving the other disciples behind, they walked toward the mountain without saying a word.

Just six days ago, Jesus had told them disturbing news—that he had to go to Jerusalem and suffer at the hands of the chief priests and the Pharisees. Jesus told them that he'd be killed. Then they embarked on this strange, silent journey.

It was unusual for this group not to be engaged in conversation. John and James were always getting into some sort of heated debate. Their passion and energy earned them the title "Sons of Thunder." Bold, brash Peter was equally known for speaking his mind, sometimes without first engaging his brain. "Fools rush in where angels fear to tread" could easily have been written for Peter. But this time it was different. Their emotions were still so strong that they didn't feel like talking.

Peter was especially troubled. After Jesus spoke of his death, Peter took him aside and rebuked him—Peter was surprised at himself for speaking to his master in such a way. And Jesus' response was equally shocking. "Get behind me, Satan!" he said to Peter, turning his blessing of just moments before into a reproof. For Peter, that hard trek up the steep mountain road was made even harder under the weight of Jesus' rebuke. The burden of his grief became a huge stone he dragged up the hill.

"Where are we going?" each man wondered to himself. Would Jesus tell them his plan? Was he running away? Was he saying goodbye before his death? The disciples didn't know. All they knew was that Jesus was leading the way and they had to follow. They had no idea what awaited them.

When they walked as far as they could, Jesus stopped, turned his face to heaven, and prayed. In a blinding moment he was changed—transfigured—before their very eyes. Moses and Elijah stood with him and the voice of God proclaimed Jesus the beloved Son. Peter, James, and John fell to their knees in worship. They'd been to the mountaintop and had encountered God.

Every so often Jesus calls us away from the crowd to spend time alone with us. He takes us out into the wilderness or up to the mountaintop just so we can be with him. It's a wonderful time and we feel special to be chosen. But it can also be a long, silent, and scary journey. What can we say to him? How can we face him after what we've done in the past? The words in our hearts can't seem to pass through our lips—we're afraid of what might come out. So, rather than take the risk, we walk along in silence.

Then the moment comes. Christ is revealed to us in new ways. We fall on our knees in awe and worship. The long, tiresome journey, the awkward silences, the guilt we felt, all are gone. Life is changed and we see Jesus for who he really is—the Son of God. The journey through the valley can be long and hard, but once we've been to the mountaintop, nothing will ever be the same.

They couldn't stay on the mountaintop. Peter wanted to, however. He blurted out, "Let's build three dwelling places—one for you, one for Moses, and one for Elijah." Peter wanted no more talk of death. How sweet it was to stay on the mountain, basking in the radiance of God's glory.

The reflected glory of the transfigured Christ shone on their faces. But as the disciples looked up at the three men in awe and wonder, suddenly a shadow came across their faces. Dark, ominous clouds seemed to swallow up the entire mountain on which they stood. The very ground shook, so that the three disciples fell to the ground in fear. Then, out of the profound depths of thunder, came the voice of God. "This is my Son, the Beloved," the voice said, "with him I am well pleased; listen to him."

The clouds dissipated as suddenly as they had come. The cowering disciples looked up toward the bright blue sky and saw Jesus standing alone before them. As Jesus bent over to help them up, he said, "Don't be afraid." The puzzled disciples brushed themselves off, and Jesus said one other thing. "Don't tell anyone what you have seen," he warned, "until the Son of Man is risen from the dead."

There was too much going through their heads—the Son of Man rising from the dead . . . Elijah! "Elijah," they wondered aloud. "Isn't Elijah to come before the Messiah?" "Yes," Jesus replied. "He has come and the world did not recognize him. And now it's time for the Son of Man to suffer and die." At that moment, Jesus began to lead them back down the mountainside.

The walk back was as silent as the walk up, but this was a different kind of silence. The three disciples didn't think so much about themselves. They thought instead about Jesus and what would come next. They wanted so desperately to understand what Jesus was saying, but all this talk about dying and rising from the dead was too complicated and strange.

The disciples had turned a corner and were embarking on a new direction in their journey. The path they were following was now leading them in another direction. Though they were returning home by the same road, their interior journey had changed. Though they'd soon be back where they started—with the same friends, in the same town—their minds had been unsettled, and they were seeing things in a new way.

Mountaintop experiences with God are wonderful. We sit in awe in the presence of God's glory, basking in the holy radiance, our faces reflecting the light of God's countenance. These experiences are so wonderful that we—just like Peter and James and John—want to stay there forever. Whether the wonderful experience happens in Sunday worship, at a weekend retreat, or in the fellowship of friends, we want to dwell there. We want to cling to what brings us closer to God.

The mountaintop, however, isn't a place to dwell. It's a place to encounter God and then get on with life. The mountaintop is a refueling station that empowers us to go back into the world and do the hard work of building the kingdom. And if we get too comfortable and don't want to move on, God comes along and gives us a little shove. The cloud rolls in and from out of the thunder comes the voice that says, "Listen to my Son."

As you walk this meditation, reflect on the times you had to walk down from the mountain. What was that like? Remember all the feelings—loss, fear, excitement, anticipation. What was it like to encounter your friends and family members who hadn't been to the mountain? How did others deal with your transfiguration? Did they scoff, or were they excited for you? Jesus told his disciples to be quiet until the time came to speak. What is the benefit of not rushing down the mountain and immediately sharing all that's happened?

Whenever you find yourself on the mountaintop, remember that you'll need to travel back home. The journey home may be even more important than the road that led you up the mountain, because this is the journey that leads to God's future for you.

The Third Movement:
Walking to the Cross

Lent

Peter (Matthew 26:31–35; 26:69–75)

"I don't know him!" As the last echo made its way through the corridors surrounding Caiaphas's courtyard, the cock crowed the arrival of a new day. For Peter, it was the dawning of the worst day of his life. He realized that he'd done the unthinkable. He had denied Jesus.

Peter ran into the darkness, trying to hide himself before the first rays of light could find him. He ran into back alleys and dark corners, but no matter where he ran, he couldn't hide—from himself or from the terrible truth that Jesus saw but he couldn't. "Before the cock crows, you will deny me three times," Jesus had said. Peter's quick response burned in his mind, "Never, Lord! I would die first!" How he wished he would. Overcome with despair, Peter stumbled into a back alleyway and collapsed. When he came to, Peter had no idea of how long he had been there. Stumbling to the street, he asked passers-by what had happened. They told him that three criminals had been taken to Golgotha to be crucified. With all the energy he could muster, Peter ran to his friend. But by the time he reached the hill, nearly everyone had gone. He saw Mary and John and a few other women at the foot of Jesus' cross. He wanted to go to his rabbi and friend, but he couldn't. He couldn't kneel next to Jesus' mother after denying him. So he stood at a distance—praying for some kind of miracle, some kind of sign, pleading with God, asking "Why?"

Almost in answer to his question, Jesus spoke, "Father, forgive them." Jesus, who had taught his disciples to love their neighbor as themselves, to turn the other cheek, and to walk the extra mile, was asking his father to forgive those who crucified him. Jesus forgave those who whipped him, those who drove the nails in his hand, and those who denied even knowing him. "I've done the worst thing imaginable," thought Peter, "And Jesus forgives even me." Peter, overwhelmed by God's love, dropped to his knees a changed man.

Peter had denied Jesus. He'd declared before a courtyard bustling with people that he had nothing to do with Jesus, his rabbi and his friend. Was his betrayal any worse than that of Judas? They both ran away into the night. Their anguish and shame was so great they both wanted to die. We know that one of them did and one of them didn't. What was the difference? Judas let his sin separate him from God. Peter turned to God with all his brokenness. Peter was able to turn to the cross and, in doing so, to receive the forgiveness of Christ. Peter faced what he'd done. Judas did not.

As you journey with Christ, there will be times when you let him down, deny him, and even betray him. But you have a choice. You can run and hide yourself from God, which ultimately means that you hide from God's love and grace. Or you can go to the cross and let Jesus clean the slate. Though you may still have to live with the consequences of your actions in this world, God's grace releases you. Your shame and your guilt will be gone. It will be the dawn of a new day, a new way.

Jesus died. And for Peter, so did the dream—his dream of working with the disciples, alongside Jesus, for a new Israel. This wasn't what he'd imagined. Who could have imagined this?

Jesus was taken down from the cross and laid in his mother's arms. Joseph of Arimathea was there, helping. Jesus was in good hands. They didn't need Peter. Peter knew he had other work to do. He had to find the rest of the disciples and make sure they were safe. Turning his face back toward Jerusalem, he began the journey to find his friends.

The walk down the hillside began slowly and arduously. His grief engulfed him as the Sea of Galilee had engulfed him the night he stepped out of the boat. It seemed like a lifetime ago. The night had been dark and overwhelming, but Jesus had reached into the darkness and pulled him out of the water to safety. "O you of little faith," Jesus had said, "Why do you doubt?" But today Jesus wasn't here to pull him out of the darkness. Jesus was gone. Resonating in his head, though, Peter still heard the words: "O you of little faith, why do you doubt?"

Faith. That was it, Peter thought. "I must not lose faith in what Jesus taught us," he told himself. His pace began to pick up. He no longer plodded down the hillside. With each step he moved more quickly and more surely. He'd find his friends and rally them back together. He'd bring them back to the place where Jesus shared his last meal with them. Together they'd return to the upper room and wait. Peter wasn't sure what they'd wait for, but somehow he knew that the answer would come.

The day began with Peter devastated and adrift. The day ended with Peter living up to his name—*Petra*, the rock. Jesus was gone but he had left his teachings. The disciples must come together and remember all that Jesus had taught and said.

When we turn from the cross after leaving our sins at the feet of Christ, it's not uncommon to still feel the weight of their burden. We've confessed, we've repented, and we've been assured that God forgives us, yet there are times when our minds are so full of the pain of what we have done that the grief lingers. If we continue to carry that pain with us, it will lead us back into more sin—the sin of faithlessness. Our refusal to let go of the pain exposes our lack of faith that God has truly forgiven us and set us free.

The journey back from the cross is our time to incorporate our new reality. We walk slowly at first, but then, as we feel the lightness of God's grace, our pace begins to quicken. Soon, we're almost running back to find our friends and loved ones so we can start again. New beginnings are the most wonderful things, but they don't always come easily.

Barabbas (Matthew 27:15–26)

"Set him free!"

Barabbas couldn't believe his ears. The Roman governor was actually letting him go.

When guards brought him out of his cell that morning, Barabbas was prepared to die. His only regret was that he couldn't kill more Romans first. His band of zealots couldn't overthrow Rome, but each attack, each dead Roman, sent the message that the Jews would never give in.

Instead of leading Barabbas to his crossbeam, however, they led him to the gate. The soldiers pushed him out with so much force that he fell into the dirt. "Jewish scum," they called him. "It looks like they've caught a bigger fish than you." Later, as he stood before the riotous crowd, he learned that the bigger fish was Jesus.

Barabbas knew who Jesus was. He'd checked him out. He'd heard rumors about miracles and such. Some even said this Jesus might be the Messiah. The very thought made Barabbas laugh. Jesus didn't act or speak like a warrior-king. Instead of talking about driving the

Romans out, Jesus talked about loving those who persecute you. Instead of killing his enemies, Jesus told his disciples to turn the other cheek. He even told the Pharisees that they should pay Caesar what belongs to Caesar. Jesus, the Messiah? Barabbas didn't think so.

But something bothered Barabbas. Why did the council and their henchmen want Jesus dead? What kind of threat was he? What made Jesus so dangerous? Barabbas had to know more. He had to see this through. Barabbas joined the crowd and followed Jesus as he made his way to Golgotha.

Barabbas walked the way of the cross. He saw Jesus stumble. He was there when the Romans drove the nails into Jesus' hands and feet—nails that had been meant for him. As they hoisted him up in the air, Barabbas couldn't help but feel that Jesus was dying for him. "It should be me on that cross," Barabbas thought. "I'm the murderer. I'm the guilty one, not Jesus."

The thought of another person dying in our place is almost more than we can comprehend. Imagine being alive only because someone else had to die. Imagine what it would be like to owe your every breath to someone who died for you. Would each breath mean more to you? Would your life be one of total and constant gratitude?

What would your response be to the person who had done this for you? Would you honor that person's name with praise and adoration? Repayment would be impossible, of course—saving a life is a debt that can never be repaid. It's the ultimate gift.

As you walk this meditation, reflect on what Barabbas might have felt as he walked behind Jesus. Try to experience his feelings as he stood at the foot of the cross—the cross that should have been his. Now think about Jesus dying on the cross for you. Look into the eyes of Christ. Hear the words, not from Pilate, but from God: "You are free!"

Barabbas had walked up the hill an angry man. He had every right to be. His was a righteous anger. He lived in an occupied land. His people were oppressed. His religious values were being compromised. He did the only thing he thought possible. He fought back. He became a zealot. He murdered in the name of Israel and in the name of God.

But what he witnessed that day changed all that. He witnessed a love so strong and pure that it overcame hatred and anger. Barabbas realized that true power doesn't come from the sword but from the heart. He realized that the power to forgive, to embrace, is the greatest power of all. Even Rome would succumb to that power. No ruler, no force on earth could resist that transforming love.

Barabbas joined the few remaining mourners staggering down the hillside. He was sad and confused, grieving over a man he had never actually met. He felt he'd lost an old friend. Yet even in his grief, Barabbas felt a sense of hope. He walked away a freer man, a lighter man. "Let's see what tomorrow brings," he thought, as he walked back from the cross.

What does it mean to be free—totally and completely free? What would that mean for you? Imagine the cross of Christ in the center of the labyrinth. Name everything you want to be free of and then lay it all down at the foot of the cross. Perhaps it's a whole long list of things. Maybe for today it's just one big thing holding you captive. Whatever it is, just lay it down, turn your back, and walk away. Don't look back over your shoulder. Keep your eyes on the journey that lies ahead of you.

With each step, feel yourself getting lighter. The heaviness of your burden fades into a memory. Let God's love begin healing the wounds left by the chains that bound you. Move with freedom. Let the joy of being truly free flow through your entire body. Christ has set you free and you're going home.

Simone Of Cyrene (Mark 15:21)

Simon stared into the angry eyes of the Roman soldier. Terror gripped his throat as his brain scrambled for options. "How could this be happening?" he wondered.

The journey couldn't have had a better beginning. They had set sail from the African coast one beautiful morning. Simon was taking his two sons, Rufus and Alexander, on their first pilgrimage to Jerusalem for Passover. The bustling city of Cyrene lay behind them, with a clear sky and the blue green water of the Mediterranean ahead. This would be a journey they'd never forget.

The ship stopped in Alexandria to pick up more passengers and cargo. Once again they set sail—this time for Joppa. The boys loved the water; they'd grown up on the coast. Simon was part of a group of Greek-speaking Jews who had settled in Cyrene, and it had been more than fifteen years since he'd been to the great temple in Jerusalem. He was as excited as his boys.

Landing in Joppa, they'd prepared for their thirty-five mile trek to Jerusalem. There was a constant stream of caravans between the two cities, especially with the coming of Passover. The land portion of their trip was a bit more demanding than the sea voyage, but it was still full of wonder and excitement. At last, they'd arrived in the Holy City of Jerusalem. Simon told the boys, "The best is yet to come!"

All that excitement faded as Simon found himself in the midst of something more horrible than he could have imagined. "No!" he desperately screamed, "I have sons. I can't leave them."

"Don't argue with me," the soldier scowled. "Pick up that cross or die."

Simon looked down at the man lying bloody and beaten on the pavement. He was obviously a criminal on his way to be executed. Simon could see the man was in no condition to continue up the steep hill carrying the heavy piece of wood that would become part of his cross. There was little skin left on his bare shoulders. As Simon looked at the man, their eyes met. He expected to see anger or fear, but instead he saw tenderness and compassion. Simon's heart was nearly broken. There was only one thing he could do. He picked up the cross of Jesus.

Life was good for Simon. Everything was as it should be. His future and that of his sons was bright and full of promise. Simon knew where he was going and his path was straight. Then, without warning, that path took a sudden turn. He came face-to-face with the suffering Christ who asks us to pick up the cross and follow him.

Remember what it was like to walk along, secure and confident in your path. Things were going well and, quite frankly, you didn't put much thought into God's plan. Now remember a time when your confidence was shaken. Something happened that made you look right into the face of Christ. It was neither sweet nor pretty. It was hard and real and compelling. You wanted to run away, but you couldn't. Your heart was moved. "If only," you thought, "if only I could take that burden from him." The burden that Christ carried was the sin of the world. Your sins are there. You can't take them back, but you can understand the weight of your sin. Look at the face of Jesus as he carries your sin. He doesn't condemn you. He looks at you with love, tenderness, and compassion.

Simon had managed to make it to the top of the hill. He bore the weight of the wooden beam as well as that of Jesus, who could barely stand, let alone walk on his own. Simon dropped the beam to the ground and then lowered Jesus as gently as he could. His body ached from the physical pain it had endured, but even more painful were the emotional wounds inflicted as he walked the way of the cross. As he lay there next to Jesus, Simon could still feel the jeering of the crowd and the cruelty of the soldiers tear at his spirit.

Yet in the midst of all that pain and humiliation, there was Jesus, leaning on him. When the crowd got too loud or the load seemed to heavy, Jesus would look into Simon's eyes with a look that said, "I understand." In those moments Simon found new strength to carry on. Every time he wanted to quit or give up, Jesus' face gave him courage.

Now it was over. The guards kicked Simon aside in their eagerness to get on with their gruesome task. Crouching there in the dust, Simon watched as the soldiers grabbed the arms of Jesus and pulled him to the beam. Stretching his arms as far as they could go, they drove nails into his hands, first one side, then the other.

Grabbing the beam, the soldiers dragged Jesus over to an even longer beam. First they nailed two beams together in the shape of a huge cross, then they took the feet of Jesus and nailed them to the wood. Together the soldiers hoisted the cross high into the air and dropped it into a pre-formed base that had been dug into the ground.

Throughout this process of excruciating inhumanity, Simon remained, watching Jesus' face. When they raised Jesus up, Simon stood so that he could get closer. He stood for what seemed like an eternity, until something else caught his attention. Two small hands reached out to take his. Looking down, he saw his sons, Rufus and Alexander.

"It's a miracle," he thought. How else could two small boys make their way through the crowd to find him here? God had watched over his sons and delivered them, just as he had delivered the Israelites from the hands of the Egyptians during Passover.

Sobbing and frightened, the boys asked what had happened. "A sacrifice," Simon said. "A sacrifice."

When we're carrying our cross, when we're being spat upon and jeered at, the loving face of Christ gives us strength. His eyes tell us that he knows our pain and suffering because he's been there. His eyes let us know that there's hope. Though we're tired and near exhaustion, when we focus on his face, we find new strength to carry on. As you walk this meditation and feel the weight of the cross on your back, feel Christ's presence, too. Feel his arms around you. Feel his heart beating with yours. The burden isn't gone, but with Christ at your side, it's somehow easier to bear. When the road seems long and unbearable, look into Jesus' eyes. Let his strength flow through you. He's gone this way before. He will lead you through to new life on the other side.

Mary (John 19:25b–20:1)

Mary didn't want to walk this path. Nobody would. But she had no choice. She walked alongside her son to his death.

Mary knew that the promise of Jesus would bring pain. All those years ago, Simeon had told her, "A sword will pierce your heart." What she had to watch her son endure, however, was much more than that. The sword cut through her entire body, ripping and tearing at every bone and muscle. She wanted to scream and make them stop. She wanted to run and pick him up as she used to. She wanted to die in his place so that he could live. But all she could do was follow and watch.

Two things kept Mary going on this journey: her faith in God's promises and Jesus' youngest disciple, John. Mary didn't understand how God could work in and through all this hatred and suffering, yet experience had shown her that God would always be there. God's promises had sustained her all of her life. She relied on those promises, she trusted in them, and she would not abandon them now.

Without John, Mary couldn't have endured this day. When the pain became too much for her to bear, John was there, holding her up, encouraging her to keep going. John cleared the way for her to make it through the crowd. Her own strength wasn't sufficient—she needed a helper. God provided John.

The path ended at Golgotha, but the journey was far from over. Mary still had to see the last vestiges of clothing stripped from her son. She had to see him nailed to the cross and lifted into the air. She had to watch her son, already beaten and bloodied, die by the most barbaric form of execution the world could think of. How could a mother bear to witness such a horror? How could a mother not be there for her child who was suffering?

The hardest thing to do is to bury a child. All parents pray to be spared that agony. It doesn't matter if the child is ten or fifty. When a child dies, a part of the parent dies, too. The memories, the dreams, the hopes, and all the things the child represented are no longer the same. The parents' reality is changed forever. Their very existence is radically redefined.

Take care in walking this meditation. If you've lost a child, go to whatever depths help you. The loss may have come through death, debilitating illness, drugs, mental illness, or a broken relationship. If you haven't experienced this type of loss, reflect on any feelings of loss and grief you have had. Lest the emotions become too over-whelming, try to focus not so much on the feelings of grief, but rather on those things that carried you through your time of grief. Reflect on God's promises. How did you feel God's presence? Where did you encounter unexpected grace?

Think also about the people who helped you through the pain and grief. Remember what it was like to have someone hold you when you couldn't stand the pain any longer. Those friends and loved ones were the loving arms of God. Even Mary, the blessed mother of our Lord, needed the strength of someone else.

They took the body of Jesus and laid him in the arms of his mother. The blood from his torn body seemed to be everywhere. His blood and her tears mingled together with the dirt to form clumps of red clay that clung to her robes. Mary was too exhausted to weep. The pain was there, along with a sense of relief that it was over. Her beloved son didn't have to suffer anymore. Mary turned him over to his Father in heaven.

It was getting dark. John begged Mary to let Joseph of Arimathea takes Jesus' body for burial. She placed one last kiss on her son's forehead as they lifted him out of her arms and placed him in a clean linen wrap. Joseph was concerned that there wasn't enough time to anoint the body properly, because Jesus had to be placed in the tomb before sunset. Mary Magdalene said she would come back after the Sabbath with myrrh and anoint his body properly.

"Myrrh," thought Mary, "as it was foretold by the magi." Her mind flashed back to the time when the strange men had come bearing gifts of gold, frankincense, and myrrh. "How strange," she had thought at the time, "funeral oil as a baby gift."

John lifted Mary to her feet and helped her follow behind her son to his burial place. Jesus, wrapped in the shroud, was placed in Joseph's newly hewn tomb as the last few rays of light disappeared behind the hill. Joseph came up to Mary, touched her lightly on the arm, and bestowed a blessing. "Woman," he said, "may God bless you now and always."

A memory of her cousin Elizabeth flashed in her mind. "Hail, O favored one!" Elizabeth had said. "Blessed are you among women." Favored one? Blessed? Mary couldn't even think in those terms. She turned, grabbed John's arm, and started her walk back to the city. With heavy feet and a broken heart, she walked while her mind whirled and her emotions churned inside her. Faintly at first, from way back somewhere almost forgotten, she began to hear a song.

He has looked with favor on the lowliness of his servant.
Surely, from now on all generations will call me blessed.

The song became clearer and stronger the further she walked.

For the Mighty One has done great things for me,
and holy is his name.
His mercy is for those who fear him

> from generation to generation.
> He has shown strength with his arm;
> he has scattered the proud in the thoughts of their hearts.
> He has brought down the powerful from their thrones,
> and lifted up the lowly;
> he has filled the hungry with good things,
> and sent the rich away empty.
> He has helped his servant Israel,
> in remembrance of his mercy,
> according to the promise he made to our ancestors,
> to Abraham and to his descendants forever. (Luke 1:49–55)

On the worst day of her life, Mary sang her Magnificat, her song of praise. She knew that what God started almost thirty-three years earlier was not over yet. God's promise was yet to be fulfilled.

When we've lost it all—or when it just seems that way—how do we respond? Do we turn our backs and go home, solemnly declaring that we won't ever be hurt again? Do we lash out at the world, screaming and crying and declaring how unfair it all is? Does the plea "Why me?" become the only sound from our lips? How unlike Mary we are. She lived through things that most of us could never imagine, yet she did not curse the world, her luck, or her God. What she did was remember. She remembered God's presence. She remembered God's promise. She remembered who she was.

Carry those losses you've experienced with you on this meditation. Hold them up to God and ask God to open your eyes. Look for times when you saw God in your pain. Look for God's presence in those who surrounded you in your grief.

Now take time to listen to God. What promises did God make to you? What does Scripture say that you can always rely on? God doesn't promise that we'll never know grief or pain or sorrow. God only promises that we won't go through it alone. God is always with us, guiding us and encouraging us. God gave us the Son to set us free from sin and death. God gave us the Holy Spirit as our comforter and teacher. God gave us one another as companions on this journey of life. God is faithful and God is there. Open your eyes to see and your heart to know.

John (John 13:1–25; 19:25b–27)

The events of the night were still reeling in John's head. He couldn't make sense of anything. He and Jesus and the disciples had been preparing for Passover, safely hidden away in the upper room of Mark's house. As they reclined at the table, eating, John remembered leaning over and placing his head on Jesus' chest. John felt Jesus' breath on the top of his head. The warm breath was steady and calm. Jesus' heart beat strongly, perhaps a little harder than normal, but John thought it was just the excitement of celebrating Passover in Jerusalem.

After supper, Jesus washed their feet. It seemed odd to have the master serve them in such a way, but Jesus said it was a lesson they all had to learn. It was uncomfortable and poignant at the same time. Jesus spoke of many things. He told them that he was leaving them a gift—peace of mind and heart. He told them to abide in God's love. "I command you," he said, "love each other in the same way I love you." Then Jesus prayed. After the prayer was done, he led the disciples out across the Kidron valley and into a grove of olive trees. There, at Gethsemane, the horror began.

John could still taste the terror in his mouth at the arrest. He remembered that they'd tried to fight, but Jesus told them to put down their swords. Guards seemed to be everywhere, in any case, so what else could they do but run away? Maybe if they got away, they reasoned, they could find help. John ran out of the garden and back to Mark's house. Surely anyone who could get away would regroup there. But no one came. John waited until daybreak, then went to find out what news he could. When he heard that Jesus was being taken to Pilate, he went back to the house to tell the women. "Stay here," he pleaded, "I'll find out what I can." But they weren't so easily deterred.

So it was that John, Mary, and a few other women were the only disciples who witnessed Jesus' trial. John became a guardian, watching over Mary as they followed the bruised and beaten Jesus through the streets of Jerusalem. John was clear and focused, knowing that he had to protect Mary. There were moments, of course, when his mind recoiled from his task. But when he'd catch a glimpse of Jesus falling or being struck by a soldier, waves of guilt, shame, and grief almost overwhelmed him. "If I had stayed and fought," he thought, "maybe this wouldn't be happening." But it was happening. All John could think about was how he'd failed Jesus. Tears of remorse burned his eyes. Each step reminded him that he was a failure. Then, just as quickly, a sigh or a stumble from Mary would bring him back. He didn't have time to think about his failure. He had to be strong for Mary.

As you walk this meditation with John, offer your failures to God. Reflect on times when you let someone down. Remember your thoughts of "not being good enough." Now, lay those thoughts down. Don't carry them with you one more step—they won't help you do what God asks of you. If John had focused on his failures, he couldn't have been there for Mary. The past was in the past. John couldn't do anything to change what had happened, but he could do something now. He could help Mary. That was all God was asking of him—nothing more.

You are human and not God. Only God is perfect. You will make mistakes. You will let people down. You will hurt and will be hurt by others. God doesn't want you to wallow in your past mistakes. That's why God forgives us! Forgive yourself as Jesus forgives you.

Jesus had preached to thousands. He'd healed hundreds. He'd discipled dozens. He was part of a big extended family. Yet only five people came to stand at the foot of his cross—four women and a youth barely old enough to be called a man. These were the only ones strong enough to go all the way to the end with him, a small following for the King of the Jews.

A war was raging inside John. "Where," he anguished, "are the others? I can't do this alone."

John was the youngest of the Twelve, and sometimes they treated him more like a kid brother than a fellow disciple. He was teased like any younger sibling, but he was also sheltered. The others always made sure that John was taken care of. Even Jesus seemed to have a special place in his heart for John. Though he sometimes protested, John actually liked being the "baby" of the family. As much as a disciple of Christ could be, John was a little bit spoiled.

But now the time had come for John to grow up. His naiveté had been nailed to the cross with Jesus, and he saw the teachings of his master in a different light. John began to understand what Jesus meant when he talked about love. Love was something more than the brotherly friendship they shared. Love was more than the good feelings he shared with the other disciples these past three years. Love was something deeper and more profound. Love, he realized, is the center of all things.

As he looked up at Jesus, John was transfigured. His eyes revealed the change that was happening inside of him. "I understand," his gaze seemed to say. "I finally understand."

At that moment, Jesus spoke. "Mother, behold your son," he said. He turned to John and said, "Behold your mother."

John understood and accepted Jesus' words. From that day forward he was no longer the "baby." He had become a man with the important responsibility of looking after the mother of Jesus. This was his new path, his new journey.

All of us have experiences that cause us to grow up a bit—events that change us or hurts that take away our naiveté. There comes a time when we can no longer hide behind innocence. We are called to step up and take responsibility.

Reflect upon a time when you were shocked out of complacency. Don't dwell on the event—that just focuses on the pain. Focus instead on the empowerment you felt in stepping up to the new challenge or the new reality. As you walk, begin moving with more intention. Be a person on a mission. Fan the flames of the fire that were once kindled in you. Feel the heat. Let the warmth energize you.

Growing up can be painful. Staying innocent and carefree is tempting. But growing up brings understanding, knowledge, and a deeper capacity for love.

The Roman Soldier (Mark 15:37–39)

He was a good Roman soldier. He'd advanced to captain without any family connections to pave the way. This tour of duty found him in Judea, where he'd been assigned to Pilate's palace company. Like most of the other soldiers, he hated it there—it was considered one of the worst postings in the empire. The locals handled most of their own problems, while the soldiers mostly dealt with those who threatened Roman authority—the zealots, freedom fighters, and the like. To the Romans, these rabble-rousers were thorns in their side. And from what was being said about this Jesus, the soldiers figured he was a very big thorn indeed. The captain saw Jesus as just one more in a long line of Jewish troublemakers. Nothing special about this one.

The captain was a little surprised during the arrest when Jesus hadn't even put up a fight. It was almost as if he'd been expecting them. They led Jesus from the garden to the high priest's house, where the Romans weren't allowed. Under his breath, the captain had muttered, "We're good enough to arrest their criminals, but we aren't good enough to set foot in a Jewish home."

Once the Jews were through with Jesus, they'd thrown him outside to the Romans. "Take him to Pilate," was all they had so say. So the soldiers did. Again the captain had thought it strange that Pilate didn't seem to want to have anything to do with this man. Pilate tried to release him, but the crowd was adamant. Pilate had ordered the soldiers to flog Jesus. They'd used the normal tool—a lead-tipped leather whip with bits of bone and metal embedded in the leather. It made most men beg to die. Some did. But not Jesus. He was strong and silent.

His silence only seemed to goad the other soldiers. After the scourging they'd placed thorn branches on his head in the shape of a crown and wrapped him in some old, dirty, purple cloth. As they'd spun Jesus around and around, the soldiers had taken turns spitting on him and striking him.

Unable to take it any more, the captain had yelled, "Stop! Enough." Doing your job was one thing, but this sadistic mockery was too much, even for him. The captain had helped Jesus up and led him back to Pilate.

Pilate, seeing the kingly mockery, had shouted to the people, "Here is your King!" The crowd started chanting, "We have no king but Caesar. Crucify him." One of the Jewish holy men had said, "Our laws demand that he die because he said he was the Son of God."

The captain felt his stomach turn. "Nonsense," he'd thought to himself. "Only a Roman could be a son of one of the gods." Yet he'd sensed something more was going on when Pilate washed his hands of the affair and said, "So be it."

The captain did what he'd done so many times before. The prisoner was directed to pick up his own instrument of death and torture, then marched through the streets of town to a hill known as the "the skull." Throughout the trial, the taunting, and the torture, the captain had been amazed that Jesus never broke—he never begged for mercy and never cursed the Romans as all the others had, not even when the captain ordered the nails driven into his outstretched hands. The captain was accustomed to seeing pain and agony. He was also used to seeing fear and hatred spew out from the condemned. But he never saw hatred or fear in Jesus.

After he'd been hung on the cross, Jesus looked down on those who tortured him and prayed, "Father, forgive them, for they don't know what they are doing." The captain looked at Jesus in amazement. After all this, Jesus asks that we be forgiven? Surely, the captain thought, Pilate was right when he said that he could find no fault in this Jesus. The man had to be innocent.

Walking with the soldier is difficult. We don't want to associate ourselves with those who actually killed Jesus. We may think to ourselves, "I have sin and brokenness in my life, but I'm not like them. I wouldn't inflict such pain on Jesus, or spit in his face, or actually drive the nails into his hands."

Really? Whose sins caused this suffering? Jesus was sinless. Don't we spit into the face of Jesus every time we turn our backs on his love and grace? Every time we treat Jesus as just another man, we mock him. We call him "King" and "Lord," but we don't mean it any more than did the Roman soldiers.

As you take this walk to Calvary, accept the truth that there's just as much Roman soldier in you as there is Mary or John or Simon. You've rejected Jesus, mocked him, betrayed him, and even crucified him. Your hands are no different than those that wielded the hammer that nailed Jesus to the cross.

Come to grips, also, with the all-forgiving love of Christ. Jesus never cursed the hands or the people who crucified him. He forgave them just as he forgives us. He holds us up to the Father even when we're in the midst of the worst possible sin because he loves us that much. No matter what you've done, to God or to others, there is always forgiveness at the cross.

The Roman captain had never questioned the guilt of those he crucified. Of course they were guilty—they were all convicted in a fair trial! It made it easier for him to do his job. He didn't have to think. But this one was different. Jesus' manner, his words, his very eyes compelled the captain to think about what he was doing. How could anyone look on this man and believe him guilty?

The captain, bewildered and shaken by what he'd witnessed, continued to stare at Jesus as he gasped for air on the cross. As he stood there, he noticed a change in the sky. Dark clouds began to gather overhead and block the sun and thunder rumbled through the clouds and over the surrounding hills. For almost three hours, every other sound of nature was virtually silent. Everything seemed to be hushed and waiting. After what seemed like forever, Jesus broke the silence with a loud cry: "It is finished." And then his body went limp. Suddenly a thunderbolt cracked and released a mighty wind. The skies opened up and poured down rain as if the heavens themselves were crying over this man's death. From deep within the bowels of the earth, the ground itself began to rumble and shake.

The captain needed to get his men off the hill. He knew that breaking the legs of the crucified would make the condemned go limp, thus allowing the fluids to enter their lungs and hasten their death, so he ordered it to be done. One guard, seeing that Jesus already appeared dead, ran a spear into his side. Out flowed blood and water. The task was done. Jesus was dead.

There, in the middle of a tempest, on a hill far away from his home, a Roman captain—who'd never before laid eyes on Jesus—made a startling proclamation, "Truly this man was God's Son."

The captain made sure that Jesus was pulled down from the cross, and then watched the family wrap him in a linen shroud and take him away. With the hill emptied, the captain gathered his troops and ordered them back to the city. On the march home, his head was filled with one burning question: Who was this man, Jesus? He was determined to find out. The captain didn't understand why or how, but this day had changed him. He had to find the meaning of what had happened. It became his quest.

Every day he spent in far-off Judea, the captain would wake up and wonder: Why me and why here? He'd a good enough life, with some power and a certain status. His needs were met. He had adequate pay, comrades to be with, and a job to do. But the fact remained that he hated Judea and the demands of his work. Now he realized that if it weren't for those things, he'd never have encountered Jesus. A simple Roman soldier stationed in a backwater country had witnessed God's mighty act of salvation.

Are there days you feel trapped in your life? Are there days you wonder why God placed you where you are? "God," we may cry, "this is the pits. Get me out of here!" We may experience long days filled with tedium and days filled with pain and agony. Like the Roman soldier, however, perhaps we've been put in these places for a specific purpose. God may have something for us to do or something for us to learn.

On this meditation, walk in your mind through those places from which you want to escape. See what's going on around you. Don't turn your eyes away from something that's difficult to watch. Instead, look at what's happening around the situation. Look for the details you might be missing. Who else is there? What are they doing? What's happening in the environment? Start looking for signs of God. The sign you see may not be as profound as an earthquake or a tempest, but God is still there for you to see. As bad as things may seem, you're there—in that particular place—to witness God's mighty act of salvation. Be alert; be on guard. God is getting ready to use you.

The Fourth Movement:
Walking in the Truth

Easter

Mary Magdalene (Matthew 28:1–10, Luke 24:1–12, Easter Morning)

Mary Magdalene was the only one moving about in the pre-dawn darkness. She hadn't slept much the past two nights since Jesus had been laid in the tomb. Her mind wouldn't rest; and when her body finally succumbed to exhaustion, she was tormented by fitful dreams of Jesus' torture and death. But now the Sabbath was over and she could finish the final act of devotion for her Lord.

After gathering the oils and spices she needed for a proper burial ritual, she awakened Mary, the mother of James, and Salome. The women silently headed for Jesus' tomb before the first rays of light began to make their way over the hills. They scurried through the streets as the city began to come alive around them. By the time they reached the hills in which the tombs were carved, morning was already beginning to chase away the darkness.

As they turned down the path toward Jesus' borrowed tomb, the earth shuddered, throwing them to the ground. Looking up, they saw the great stone that had covered the entrance to the tomb rolled away. On the ground, surrounding the opening, lay the Roman guards, as motionless as death. The other Mary and Salome started to flee in terror, but Mary Magdalene hadn't come this far to run away. She stepped up to the tomb looking for Jesus. What she saw was a young man in dazzling white robes who spoke to her. "I know that you are looking for Jesus who was crucified," he said. "He is not here. He is risen. Go. Tell his disciples they will see him in Galilee."

Mary Magdalene called out to the other women, "Jesus is risen! He's alive!" Turning in haste to catch up with the others, she ran into a man standing off to the side, knocking herself to the ground. Lying there, dazed and blinded by the rising sun, she took him for the gardener and asked if he knew anything of Jesus. With a little laugh, his voice loving and familiar, he called her name: "Mary."

She recognized him instantly. With sobs and laughter, she threw her arms around Jesus' legs. "Rabbi," she cried. Jesus gently lifted her up. "Do not cling to me, Mary. There is much to be done. You must go and tell my disciples what you have seen." With those words, he departed from her.

Mary's heart had been churning with conflicting emotions when she set out for the tomb that Easter morning. Her grief was practically overwhelming. Jesus had been her rabbi, the teacher who had healed her by casting out seven demons. But he was more than just her rabbi. Abandoned by her family and friends, with no one who cared for her, Jesus had made her part of his family.

Mary was angry, too. She had every right to be. She was angry with the Romans for crucifying Jesus and she was angry with the Pharisees for having Jesus arrested in the first place. She was even angry with the men closest to Jesus, his disciples. Where were they? Why was John the only one of Jesus' disciples to be there with the women?

But whatever emotions were raging inside Mary Magdalene, she remained dedicated to Jesus. We see her amazing strength and courage. When others ran away, Magdalene stayed to do what was required. Her reward was being the first to witness the resurrection. The very first person Jesus appeared to was Mary Magdalene.

Walking in the valley of the shadow of death is not easy. There are moments when every ounce of our being screams, "Enough!" As Mary watched Jesus carry his cross, there must have been times she wanted to turn away. She knelt at the foot of his cross, fighting back the revulsion she felt throughout her body. Yet she remained. And she did more. She went back to Jesus' tomb to minister to his broken body.

For Mary, love overcame fear. The power of forgiveness overcame the horror of death. This is the message of Jesus. This is why he first appeared to Mary Magdalene. She understood the meaning of the cross even before she knew exactly what it entailed. Before any of the other disciples did so, Mary "got it."

As you walk with Mary to the tomb, think of Jesus' message of love and forgiveness. What would it take for you to really "get it"? It's what enables you to pick up your cross every day and follow him, the strength that comes from the peace of God that passes all understanding.

Mary ran to catch up with the other women. "I've seen Jesus!" she blurted out excitedly. "I've talked to him and touched him." There was no time to stand and celebrate. The women had to hurry and tell the others. They headed straight for Mark's house, which had become the disciples' headquarters in Jerusalem.

They burst inside, flinging open the doors and flooding the room with sunlight. "Jesus is alive!" Mary shouted. "He is risen and I have seen him." The entire household began to buzz. Everyone crowded around the three women, firing questions at them: "What do you mean?" "How could this be?" Mary tried to explain exactly what happened—about the earthquake, the soldiers, the man in white, and the empty tomb. She told them she'd seen Jesus, though at first she didn't recognize him.

Some of the disciples laughed at her. Some said her story was just wishful thinking. Others wondered if she wasn't still a little crazy. But not one of them believed her, no matter how hard she tried to convince them. To make matters worse, the other two women couldn't corroborate Mary's story—they'd felt the earthquake, they testified, and they'd seen the fallen guards. But they hadn't seen Jesus. It was only Mary's word, and nobody believed her.

"At least go and see for yourself," she pleaded. So Peter and John went back with Mary to see for themselves. As they approached the tomb, John ran ahead, with Peter right behind him. John, stopping at the open tomb, was afraid to look inside, but Peter didn't hesitate. He stepped in and found it empty. The linen cloths were still lying in place, but there was no Jesus. The two disciples just started turning back as Mary reached them. "He's not here, Mary," Peter said, "but that doesn't mean he's alive. It just means someone may have taken his body."

Mary slumped to the ground as the two disciples walked away. "Why won't they believe me?" she cried. Even the empty tomb wasn't enough to convince them. Standing up, Mary became resolute. "It doesn't matter if they believe me or not," she told herself. "I know Jesus is alive and he'll reveal himself when it's time." Without even dusting the dirt off her robes, Mary Magdalene walked back to the house where the disciples stayed. "He's alive," she said. "I can wait."

Remember when you had a God-encounter? Theologians call it a theophany, and it hits you right between the eyes. All of sudden, out of nowhere, you bump smack into God. Then, as often as not, you land right on your backside. You jump up, realize what's happened, and off you run to tell all your friends and family. You want to share it with everybody, but not everybody is ready to hear it. People smile at you politely and nod their heads. Sometimes you get quizzical looks, as though they're not sure what to think of you. They wonder if you've gone completely daft or possibly had a little too much to drink.

At times like these, you might have been swayed by the nay-sayers. "Maybe I was being emotional," you might think. "Maybe I just got carried away. Maybe there's a rational explanation for what happened."

Or you might have been like Mary Magdalene. You might have stood firm in your faith that what happened really was a God-encounter. Perhaps you didn't argue with your friends or try to convince them—you were happy just to live into the reality of the experience.

We are all called to witness to our experience. God is responsible for the rest. God does the convincing. Draw strength from Mary Magdalene, who was ridiculed and dismissed just because she was a woman. God turns the world upside down and does it with the lowly and least likely.

Cleopas (Luke 24:13–35, Easter Evening)

It was a full day's journey back to Emmaus, and the burden of the past two days would make the trip even more difficult. With no reason to stay in Jerusalem any longer than necessary, Cleopas and his companion started home early on the morning after Passover.

The two walked along in stunned silence for the first few hours. The events of the past two days seemed like a bad dream. All their hopes and plans for the future were killed along with Jesus.

As the sun rose in the sky and the heat of the day began to build, Cleopas couldn't keep quiet any longer. He cried out, "Why?" Turning to his companion, Cleopas pleaded, "How could this have happened?"

Once the silence had been broken, the two disciples began to share stories of Jesus. They recalled their first meeting with him—they'd known immediately that there was something different about the man. They talked about how much they'd learned from him.

They spoke of the time that Jesus sent them out as part of the seventy to preach and teach and heal. It all seemed of God. But where was God now?

The sun was beginning to lead the two travelers westward as they continued their walk. Engrossed in sorrowful conversation, they barely noticed the stranger come up beside them. "You seem to be in a deep discussion about something," the man said. "What are you so concerned about?"

Cleopas stopped abruptly. With a heavy sadness written all over his face, he replied, "You must be the only person in Jerusalem who hasn't heard about all the things that have happened there the last few days." Cleopas told the stranger about Jesus of Nazareth—a prophet, a miracle worker, and, some thought, the long-awaited Messiah. Cleopas told the stranger about Jesus' arrest, his torture, and his crucifixion. And he told the stranger that some women from their group had gone to the tomb that morning and found his body missing—an angel, they said, had told them that Jesus was alive. Two of their friends, Peter and John, had gone to see for themselves, but had seen only an empty tomb.

The stranger shook his head. "You are such foolish people!" he exclaimed. "You find it so hard to believe all that the prophets wrote in the Scriptures. Didn't they predict that the Messiah would have to suffer all these things before entering his time of glory?" Then he quoted passages from Scripture, explaining what they meant and how they pertained to Jesus.

By now the two disciples were near the end of their journey and the sun was beginning to set. They saw an inn ahead and Cleopas suggested they stop, rest, and eat. The stranger seemed to be more interested in continuing his journey, but Cleopas entreated him to stop and break bread with them.

As the three sat down to eat, the stranger took a small loaf of bread, asked God's blessing on it, broke it, then gave it to them. The two disciples looked into the eyes of the man with outstretched hands. All of a sudden, the blinding reality of the stranger's identity hit them. This man, who had walked with them and taught them, was Jesus himself!

A thousand questions flew through their minds, but before they could speak a single word, Jesus had disappeared. "Of course," Cleopas exclaimed. "Didn't our hearts burn inside us as he talked with us and explained the Scriptures?"

Sometimes it's hard to see God's presence when our dreams don't turn out as we planned. We ask ourselves, "How could God have let this happen?" We can become so devastated by our sorrow that we can't see God at work around us. Even when others tell us how they've experienced God's hand at work, we aren't affected. Our pain becomes the most overwhelming reality in our lives.

For Cleopas and his fellow disciple, Jesus himself had to open their eyes. How did Jesus do it? He did it through the Scriptures and the Eucharist. The disciples' hearts were warmed as they considered God's Word; their eyes were opened through the breaking of the bread. In times of sorrow, disappointment, and pain, we can find comfort in the Word and in worship. They are direct encounters with the Risen Christ.

Next time life doesn't work out as you planned, pick up the Bible and start reading. Read God's promises. Read about how God cared for God's people in times of trouble. Read the good news of Christ. And don't neglect your worship. Seek God in the breaking of the bread and in the prayers. Wherever two or three are gathered in God's name, Jesus assures us, God is in the midst of them.

God will not leave you alone. There may be times you won't realize God's presence right away. As it was with the disciples on the road to Emmaus, it may take you some time. But God is there, waiting to open your heart.

Jesus took the bread, blessed it, broke it, and gave it to his disciples. In that moment, the eyes of the disciples were opened and they saw Jesus for who he really was. All they had learned and experienced in their years with Jesus became clear in an instant.

That night in Emmaus, the two disciples were alive with excitement. Leaving their sadness behind, they decided they had to go right back to Jerusalem and tell the others. This was something that couldn't wait until morning. Gulping down a few bites of food, they replenished their supplies and started the long walk back to Jerusalem.

Though the road to Jerusalem was familiar, the darkness made the disciples nervous. The small oil lamps they carried only lit up the road a few feet in front of them. "What if a robber is waiting up ahead?" they wondered." Fear began to creep in and they wondered if they should have waited until morning.

But as they thought about turning back, they remembered Jesus breaking the bread. Filled with new courage and determination, they pressed forward on their journey. The good news that Jesus was alive couldn't wait.

They maintained a quick pace as they scurried along the roadway. They practically ran. Even after traveling all day, they felt no exhaustion. Time didn't seem to have any meaning and, before they knew it, they were in Jerusalem. Running up to the house where the disciples were staying, they were surprised to find the lamps burning and people awake.

Inside they saw Jesus' close disciples, the women, and others who had been with them. "Good news!" one of the people shouted. "The Lord has really risen and appeared to Peter!"

"And to us, also!" exclaimed Cleopas, who told what had happened on the road to Emmaus. Excitement sparked as they shared their experience of the Risen Lord.

At that moment—as suddenly as he had disappeared from the table at Emmaus—Jesus appeared before them in the house in Jerusalem. "Peace be with you," Jesus said. Many who hadn't seen him since his death drew back in apprehension and awe, but Jesus reassured them. "Don't be frightened," he said. "Come and touch me and see for yourselves that I am not a ghost." Jesus sat down with them and, in much the same way he had done with Cleopas and the other disciple, he opened their hearts and minds to see that he was the fulfillment of all the promises of Scripture.

Recall those times when you suddenly realized that you were in the presence of Jesus. How did you feel? Were you excited? Surprised? Frightened? Did your heart feel on fire? That's what it was like for Cleopas and the other unnamed disciple. Their hearts burned in the presence of Jesus.

What did you do after that moment passed? Was the moment so alive, so filled with excitement that you had to share the news with someone else? Could you have held it in if you tried? Let the feeling come back to you now. Remember how it felt in every part of your body. Let the energy flow through you.

Now, as you walk this meditation, feel the difference in the way you're walking. Is your body moving forward with more purpose? Is your step quicker? Spend some time just releasing this energy as you walk.

It's impossible to sustain that intense energy all the time as we witness to Christ in our lives. But it's something we can always draw on. When we feel weary in our Christian journey, we can remember how we felt when we first encountered the Risen Lord. We remember in the Eucharist, of course, but we can remember that experience at any time and in any place. When the journey gets frightening, we don't have to sit down and break bread again. All we have to do is remember. The presence of Christ is with us always. Open your heart and make room.

Saul *(Acts 9:1–19, Easter 3C)*

Saul's campaign to wipe out those blaspheming followers of Jesus was going just as he'd planned. The assault needed a memorable event to get it going, and the execution of Stephen provided just that.

It was high-profile—it attracted a lot of attention and got the crowd going. With the impetus of Stephen's arrest and execution, Saul could go throughout Jerusalem hunting down the followers of the criminal Jesus.

Once fear gripped the people, the followers were easy to find. Neighbors, friends—sometimes even relatives—turned them in. Saul would break into their homes in the middle of the night and carry them away. Now Saul was ready to move on. His next city: Damascus, where many followers of Jesus were rumored to be hiding. Saul went to the high priest and asked for letters to the synagogues in Damascus. If he found anyone there who was a follower of The Way, as these people called their cult, he'd have the authority to bind them and bring them back to Jerusalem for trial.

As Saul gathered his men and began the journey northward, he reveled in how well his plan was going. Not only was Saul serving God by destroying these blasphemers, but he was also making quite a name for himself—this much attention would certainly help his career. Who knows how far he could go? As Saul rode along toward Damascus, he felt as if he were sitting on top of the world.

Damascus was in sight and Saul could almost see his future rising before him. Suddenly, a bright and powerful light flashed from heaven. Saul's horse bolted and threw him to the ground. In the midst of the panic, a voice came from nowhere. "Saul, Saul, why do you persecute me?" the voice demanded. Saul, frightened and confused, asked, "Who are you, Lord?" The voice replied, "I am Jesus, whom you are persecuting. Now get up and go into the city and you will be told what you are to do."

Saul's men came and helped him stand. But though his eyes were open, he was completely blind. A million thoughts flashed through his mind. "Who is this Jesus? How could he have the power to do such a thing?" For the first time in his life, Saul was truly frightened. He wasn't afraid for his safety. He was afraid because everything he'd ever believed suddenly came into question. "What if," Saul thought, "I was wrong?"

The once fearsome Saul, now blind and helpless, was led by his servants into Damascus.

Most of us would never think of ourselves in the same vein as Saul. Saul was Jesus' most ardent enemy. He tracked down followers of The Way and had them killed. His goal was to blot Jesus and his followers from the face of the earth. Enemies of Christ? Killers? Not me, we say to ourselves. But what does Jesus teach us about sin? You say you have never murdered? Well, anyone who calls his brother or sister a fool is guilty of murder.

Have you ever attacked other Christians, clergy, or even the Church because you believed they weren't doing things the "right" way? Has your so-called righteous anger hurt others who have disagreed with you? At one time or another, we've each done something like that. We can say, self-righteously, that "we were defending God and the faith." But can we as easily admit that we—like Saul—also liked looking good to others? But while we wave our banner and proclaim ourselves pure and holy, we're denouncing the other side as unclean and unfit.

If this hasn't happened to you yet, it will. You'll be riding along triumphantly, feeling on top of the world, when—all of a sudden—God will come along and knock you off your high horse. Humbled, lying in the dirt, unable to see clearly, you'll hear God's voice: "I am Jesus. You are persecuting me. If you hurt the body, you hurt me."

Where is your Damascus? Where is it that you feel you need to defend Christ? On your journey to that place, don't let your heart be so hardened that you can't hear God speaking to you. The harder you keep God out, the harder it is for God to get your attention. Be attuned to God tapping you on your shoulder or you may end up on your back in the dirt.

Saul knew he'd been in the presence of the Living God. He knew that from that day forward, nothing would ever be the same. He knew little else. He didn't know what the future would hold. He didn't know how his life would change. All Saul knew was that the old life was gone and a new life lay ahead.

As he sat and waited, Saul did the only things he could do. He did what his faith had taught him. He fasted and prayed. For three days, he sat in darkness and waited for God to answer his prayers. There would be hints here and there—a vision, for instance, of a man named Ananias coming to heal his eyes. But God's plan was still hidden.

Saul called out to God. "Why are you silent?" he demanded. "What do you want from me?" But there was only stillness and more waiting. What Saul didn't know was that God was not silent. God was giving others pieces of the plan. God spoke to Ananias and told him to go to the house of Judas and find Saul of Tarsus. That's how it came to pass that Ananias found Saul, the great persecutor. And Saul, who three days earlier had been on his way to have men like Ananias killed, humbly welcomed him.

As you walk this meditation, reflect on a time when you were humbled or proven wrong. Did it turn your world upside down? Recall the feelings you experienced. Get in touch with the pain, humiliation, or sense of loss. Did you call out to God? Did God answer you in ways you wanted? How did that make you feel? Were you angry with God? Walk those feelings out. Think of Saul sitting for three days in darkness and confusion, fasting and praying. The further God felt from him, the closer he drew toward God.

Perhaps this isn't all about a past event for you. Is there some confusion in your life right now that you wish God would resolve? Do you want to know what God has in store for you? Is your cry: "Where are you and what do you want from me?" Don't run away from those feelings. Offer your sense of hopelessness or confusion to God. The further God feels from you, the more you need to draw closer to God.

Fast, pray, be intentional—but don't expect to get all the answers right away. God may give you a small vision or a dream or an insight. Hold onto it and wait for the pieces to fit together. God is working in the world around you to bring all things into clarity. Your life isn't lived in isolation. God is working in countless others and moving in their hearts as well. Like Saul, your role in God's plan may not be what you expect.

Ananias (Acts 9:1–19, Easter 3C)

Ananias was a godly man, part of the growing church in Damascus, which had been increasing rapidly, not only from new converts, but also from the influx of refugees from Jerusalem. Those who fled to Damascus told stories of the Pharisee Saul of Tarsus, who was hunting down followers of Jesus and putting them to the death. Ananias prayed daily for his fellow disciples.

One day while he was in prayer, Ananias had a vision from the Lord. The Lord called out his name and Ananias answered as the prophets of old, "Here I am, Lord."

The Lord spoke to Ananias, saying, "Get up and go to the street called Straight, and at the house of Judas look for a man of Tarsus named Saul. At this very moment he also is praying. I have given him the vision of a man named Ananias who will come and lay hands on him so that he might regain his sight."

Ananias was fearful and answered God, saying, "Lord, I have heard from many about this man who has done much evil to your saints in Jerusalem." But God assured Ananias, "Go, for he is the instrument I will use to bring my name before the Gentiles and kings and before the people of Israel. I myself will show him how much he must suffer for the sake of my name."

Ananias had sought God in prayer and God had answered him. The answer, however, wasn't what he expected. God didn't respond to Ananias's prayer by killing Saul. Instead, God asked Ananias to seek out Saul and heal him.

A godly man, Ananais set out for the street called Straight, torn by conflicting emotions. He was filled with hate for Saul—an enemy who had killed his friends. Ananias may have even wondered, "If I had to, could I kill Saul?"

Behind the hate was also fear. Ananias knew that God was with him; however, he also knew that other disciples had died at the hands of Saul. What if God were asking this of him? As much as he trusted God, fear gripped his heart as he thought of his own martyrdom.

Ultimately, what drove Ananias to seek out Saul was neither hate nor fear, but trusting obedience. Ananias trusted God. He knew that whatever God asked of him, there had to be a reason for it. God told Ananias to heal Saul, and that was all Ananias needed to know.

Pausing outside the door of Judas's house, Ananias took a deep breath, said a quiet prayer, and knocked. A man opened the door and let him in. There at the table sat Saul. His face was turned toward Ananias, but his eyes seemed clouded over. Obviously, he was blind. Ananias stepped toward Saul and placed one hand on his shoulder and the other over Saul's eyes. "My brother Saul," said Ananias, "the Lord Jesus, who appeared to you on your way here, has sent me so that you may regain your sight and be filled with the Holy Spirit." Immediately something like scales fell from Saul's eyes.

Saul blinked and rubbed his eyes. Squinting at Ananias, he replied, "My brother Ananias, I have met the Lord Jesus and have come to believe. Please, baptize me."

Recall a time when you were called outside your comfort zone, as Ananias was. How scary was it to go to someone you feared because God told you to? The last thing you wanted to do was to speak to that person, but deep inside you knew it was what God wanted. Imagine the fear in Ananias's heart as he knocked on Judas's door. His very life could have been at stake. Ananias didn't want to go at first. He argued with God, but God told him that Saul was to be the instrument that would bring the news of Christ to the Gentiles. God had a plan. In order for that plan to be accomplished, Ananias needed to go to Saul.

It involved more than just Ananias or Saul. It affected the history of the world.

If there's someone God is calling you to speak with, take courage in the story of Ananias. Your actions may not change the history of the world—but then, you never know what God has in mind. If God is indeed calling you to action, the result will be part of God's plan. Who knows? Your obedience may change the world after all. If nothing else, it will change you.

Ananias walked back home, but this time he had a companion. With him walked his former enemy—now his brother in Christ— Saul. Ananias couldn't quite believe it. The persecutor of the Church, the killer of Stephen, had actually asked to be baptized by him! Now the two of them walked side by side, talking about Jesus. "It's a miracle," thought Ananias.

Ananias was excited. This was God at work. He began to think what it would mean for the Church. The Church! How would the other believers react when he brought Saul back with him? After all, they hadn't received a vision from God. Would they believe Ananias? Would they trust Saul? Ananias knew that many would be suspicious. It wouldn't be easy to convince them.

All the way home, Ananias considered what he might say. He knew some of the refugees from Jerusalem might recognize Saul immediately, so he had to get right to the point before the crowd reacted and possibly tried to harm Saul. How ironic, Ananias thought. Here he was, planning a way to defend his worst enemy. The funny thing was that Saul was no longer his enemy but his brother. Through baptism, the two were now one, as Christ and his Church are one. Ananias relaxed. God, he felt sure, would give him the words to say.

Have you ever brought someone new to church—a friend or an acquaintance who wasn't a Christian? Statistics show that most people start attending a particular church because someone they know brings them. Friendship evangelism is still the best way to bring others to Christ.

As you walk, think about the people you know who need God's healing touch. There are your friends—those who are very much like you. You like to do the same things and have similar tastes. Now expand your thinking to include those you encounter often but don't have much in common with. Think of those who are of a different color or background, or who speak a different language. Who might be beyond your comfort zone?

What? Are you afraid to bring up the topic of God because you don't know how someone will respond? Then don't mention God. Not right away. Do what Ananias did. Offer a healing hand. Reach out to those who are hurting and blind and offer God's healing grace. When people ask you why you care, then you can let them know that it's what God asks of you.

If God gave you a vision to reach out to some specific person in friendship or invite him or her to church, wouldn't you do it? After all, God was specific in telling Ananias to go to Saul. But isn't God calling us to bring others to Christ too? Does God have to give us specific names and addresses? It's what he did with Ananias. But remember this: Ananias, praying for the deliverance and safety of all his fellow disciples, included Saul in those prayers.

Start lifting up in prayer those who are around you. Especially pray for those who seem to be lost and those who are antagonistic toward God. Identify them now and begin praying for them as you walk. Make them part of your regular daily prayer. Ask God to open doors for you so that you can minister to the people for whom you're praying. Remember, Ananias wasn't told to go and convert Saul—he was told to go and heal him. Who is God calling you to bring healing to? Start praying for those people now, even though it may seem scary at first. God will overcome your fears and give you the tools you need to carry out God's plan.

The Ethiopian Eunuch (Acts 8:26–40, Easter 5B)

The court official from Ethiopia was beginning his long journey home. His pilgrimage to Jerusalem had come to an end. Begun many months ago, his pilgrimage was filled with a desire to find spiritual answers for his life. He was desperately seeking something, although he wasn't quite sure what.

The official had studied some of the Jewish teachings. He'd been intrigued enough to take a long journey north to find out for himself what this so-called "one true god" was like. He went to the temple to find this God of the Hebrews. He was allowed to enter the temple gates, but only as far as the outer court—the court of the Gentiles, it was called. There, along with a few Greeks, Romans, and others who were not Jews, he hoped to experience the presence of God.

He learned that Gentiles could convert and become Jews. He also learned that could never happen for him. As an official in the queen's court, he'd been required to become a eunuch, and the Jews saw this as an abomination. They called him defective, unfit to become one of them. Dejectedly, he began his journey home.

But the burning desire to fill his emptiness remained. He'd learned that money and position could buy many things, even copies of Hebrew Scripture. He'd spend the trip home learning for himself about the God of the Hebrews. He unrolled the first scroll and began reading. It was written in Greek, a language he knew well. The words were easy but the meaning was difficult to discern. Here, in the book of Isaiah, the prophet wrote about a servant who offered himself as a lamb to be slaughtered. The Ethiopian wondered what the humiliation of one man had to do with God.

Over and over again he read the passages. He had a feeling that they were important, but he didn't know why. As he was reading aloud, the court official heard a voice call out to him. Looking outside his chariot, he noticed a man on foot, but the Ethiopian guards ran to stop the man from coming any closer. "Do you understand what you're reading?" the man asked. "How could I unless I had someone to guide me?" replied the eunuch. "I can guide you," the stranger replied.

With that, the eunuch asked the stranger to join him in his chariot. It was Philip, a disciple of Jesus, and he began to teach the eunuch how Jesus was the fulfillment of the prophecies found in Scripture.

The eunuch devoured Philip's words like food given to a starving man. His famished spirit began to come alive as he heard the good news of Jesus. When they came to some water alongside the road, the eunuch ordered the chariot to stop and asked Philip to baptize him. As the eunuch came up out of the water, Philip vanished. Standing alone in the water, filled with the Holy Spirit, the eunuch rejoiced in the knowledge that he was a child of the Living God.

The Ethiopian eunuch had been desperately seeking God, refusing to let anything stand in the way of his quest. Those who had the answer, however, wouldn't let him in. There were so many obstacles he had to overcome. He was a different race and a different color. He wasn't born of a Jewish mother. All of those things could have been overcome, but there was one thing that could not. He was a eunuch. The Hebrew Scriptures were clear: anyone who had been mutilated that way could never become a Jew. In the eyes of the community, the eunuch was an abomination.

But then Jesus intervened. Jesus sent an angel to his disciple Philip. The angel in turn sent Philip on a mission that would open the way of salvation to all people. Jesus didn't care who the Ethiopian was or where he came from. Jesus didn't even care if the law called the eunuch an abomination. All Jesus cared about was that he was seeking God. Jesus opens his arms to anyone who truly seeks after God.

There are so-called eunuchs all around us. There are people the Church has called unclean—even abominations. But God doesn't see any of us that way. Jesus died for each and every one of us. We are not abominations; we are the beloved children of God.

On this walk, mentally take with you those people you may have thought of as abominations. In your mind, talk with them. Listen to what they might be telling you. Is there someone for whom you can be a Philip?

Perhaps you yourself have been treated as an abomination. Remember a time when someone came to you as Philip came alongside the Ethiopian eunuch. Remember someone who told you about a loving God, someone who treated you with respect and dignity. How did that change you?

The eunuch was labeled an outsider. But no one is an outsider in God's kingdom. No one sin is any greater than another. Christ died for all. Finish this prayer walk rejoicing in the knowledge that no matter where you came from or what you've done, you are a child of the Living God.

The Ethiopian eunuch practically leapt out of the water. Those passages that had been indecipherable a few hours ago now made perfect sense. The longing that he'd felt for so long was finally satisfied. Things were so much clearer now. He understood who he was and whose he was. He belonged to God.

The royal guards ran up to their master, bringing blankets to dry him. The guards were perplexed. They wondered why their master was in the water and what happened to the stranger who had been with him. Their master, still laughing and exhilarated, tried to answer them as best he could, saying that he'd received the one true God into his heart and that his life was changed.

The guards helped their master dry off and settle back into his chariot, all the while giving each another looks that said their master must have been drinking. The eunuch knew his guards thought he was either drunk or crazy. If he had seen someone else act this way, he might have thought the same. But an amazing thing had happened to him. He hadn't been drinking and he wasn't crazy. As the stranger told him about Jesus, the eunuch knew in his heart that the story was true. He believed in Jesus as the Son of God. He received the Holy Spirit and was baptized. For now, that was all that mattered. The trip back to Ethiopia was just beginning, and the eunuch and his guards would travel together for weeks. There was plenty of time to tell them about Jesus. But for now, the eunuch settled back into his chariot, picked up another scroll, and continued reading.

Let this be a walk of pure rejoicing. Remember when you first came to know Jesus as your Lord. Let those feelings flow through you as you walk. If you feel like running or skipping, do it! Wave your hands in the air. Laugh out loud. Let the world wonder what you've been up to. There are so few times we actually just let go and rejoice in the fact that we're sons and daughters of the Most High. Let this be one of those times. Sing, laugh, cry, dance; move however the Spirit wants to move you. You are a child of the King!

The Fifth Movement: Walking in the Spirit

The Season After Pentecost

The Widow of Nain (Luke 7:11–17, Proper 5C)

A mother's loving hands rubbed the last bit of oil on her son's lifeless body. She remembered how she anointed him the day he was born and now she was anointing him on the day of his death. As she placed the linen shroud over his face, she bent down and gave him one last kiss. It was time for the procession to begin.

Four men came and placed her son's body on the bier. They lifted it up and placed it on their shoulders. Stepping out from the house, the professional mourners began to play their flutes and sing their laments. Tradition held that even the poorest of families provide two flute players and at least one singing woman. It was hard, but the mother managed to come up with enough money to pay all three.

As the procession moved out into the streets of Nain, the woman looked back at the house she'd shared with her only son. She wondered if it would be her home for much longer. Her husband had died several years earlier, and her son had been all that she had left. Now he was gone, too. With no money and no one to care for her, the woman knew this house could no longer be her home.

"But tomorrow must take care of itself," she thought. "Today I must bury my son." So the woman turned her face forward and began her march through the streets of town. The mourners wailed forth their eulogy: "What a strong young man! How sad is the death of this young man!" The eulogy and laments were meant to honor the deceased and give voice to the pain and anguish. At that moment, the last thing the woman could think about was the future and her welfare. Her only thought was that her beloved son was dead. Giving in to her grief, she began sobbing and wailing as the funeral procession made its way to the town's gate.

As the procession left the town and started up the small hill to the burial site, a man came up to the woman. "Do not weep," he said. She was taken aback. "Not weep?" she thought. "How can I keep from weeping as I bury my only son?" Without another word, the stranger touched the young man's bier. The bearers stood still. This stranger was now unclean, for he had touched the litter of a dead man. The entire crowd was stunned. The wailing stopped and silence fell around them.

It seemed like an eternity passed in just those few moments. Then, before the bewildered crowd, the stranger leaned forward and spoke to the dead man, "Young man. I say to you, rise!" As if startled out of a brief sleep, the young man sat up and pulled down his linen shroud and rubbed his eyes as they adjusted to the light. "What happened?" he asked. "Where am I, Mother?"

The bearers were so startled that they almost dropped the young man. The crowd gasped. Women screamed. The mother who had been crying with grief only seconds before was now crying with joy. She ran to her son and cradled him in her arms, all the while praising God. Soon other voices were heard in the crowd, "This man is a great prophet!" They all agreed that God had looked favorably upon them that day.

The widow wasn't seeking Jesus. She was in the middle of burying her son when Jesus found her. Perhaps she didn't even know who Jesus was. There is no indication that she or anyone else recognized him. God's healing grace came suddenly and from out of nowhere.

There are times in our spiritual journey when we're intentionally seeking God, beating on God's door, begging for a response. And there are other times when God shows up unexpectedly and unannounced. During this prayer walk, reflect on times in the past when God showed up unexpectedly in your life. What was going? Why was it such a shock to stumble on God's presence? Had you stopped looking for God? Had you given up on God? Spend time exploring why it was that God took you by surprise.

As you finish your walk, think about the future. Do you think that God will surprise you again? If we're truly living in God's presence and have faith that God is in control, then can we be truly surprised when God acts? When we're in tune with God, even miracles will begin to seem ordinary.

One minute there was only death and hopelessness. Then God stepped into the picture and brought forth new life and new possibilities.

The widow of Nain walked over to the man who had raised her son from the dead, fell at his feet, and asked him his name. "Please, sir," she demanded, "tell me who it is that brought my son back to me."

Jesus bent down and helped the widow to her feet. "Now is not the time," he said. "Go home and rejoice with your son. There will be time later to talk of such things."

The townspeople began to crowd around them, directing questions at Jesus. "Who are you? Are you the rabbi Jesus we've heard about?" They pressed in on the young man, asking, "What was it like? Tell us about the other side!"

The woman cried out, "Please let my son be. Let us go home and prepare a celebration feast." A shout went up from the crowd, "A celebration!" With that, the people began to move back toward the town. The widow and her son were almost pushed all the way back to their humble house.

Once they got there, the woman barely had any time to think of herself as she began to prepare a celebration feast. She gathered what food she had and then began cleaning the house. When she came to the bed where only hours earlier her son had died, she stopped. Bending down, she picked up the jar of myrrh she had used to anoint his body. Her son came up behind her and put his arms around her. She could still smell the oils on his skin. Slowly, a smile crept upon her face. A grin grew and grew until a gasp of air escaped from her lips. She started to laugh, gently at first, then harder, until her whole body shook. She threw her head back and laughed out loud, just like a young girl.

The widow of Nain was a poor woman with no family. She was just another of the nameless, faceless people who have lived hard lives—with one difference: she encountered Jesus who was filled with compassion, that feeling of such intense empathy that leaves you no choice but to respond to the needs of others.

As you walk, think of a time when you felt hopeless or lost. Try to remember how you felt without letting the feelings come back and overpower you. Now as you move, imagine a man standing on the path in front of you. You aren't frightened of the man. He is simply standing there, smiling at you. As you draw closer, you realize that it's Jesus, and you stop and listen to what he has to tell you. Perhaps "Stop crying," "Have no fear," or "I am with you." Now, let Jesus speak to whatever in your life that needs healing. Stand still and receive whatever Jesus has to give you.

After you've heard his words, begin walking again. This walk is different, because Christ has touched you. Walk as if you were returning home to celebrate. The past has not changed, but it no longer has the power of death over you. God has turned your mourning into dancing. Throw your head back and laugh.

The Sinful Woman (Luke 7:36–50, Proper 7C)

The woman heard that Jesus had returned to Capernaum. That very evening he'd eat dinner at the home of Simon the Pharisee. A crowd would surely gather to hear the rabbi speak. She remembered hearing Jesus speak to a huge crowd on the plain outside the city. That day had changed her life forever.

The woman remembered Jesus saying to the crowd, "Blessed are you who are poor, for yours is the kingdom of God. Blessed are you when people hate you, exclude you, and defame you for your reward is great in heaven." She also remembered his telling them not to judge or condemn one another. She couldn't believe such words could come out of the mouth of a rabbi. For most of her adult life, the woman had felt constantly judged and condemned by the rabbis and the Pharisees who told her she was unclean and unworthy of God's love. She knew she was a sinner. She knew that selling her body for money was against God's law. But what choice did she have? Her husband had cast her off with a writ of divorce. Her father was dead and she had no male relatives to take her in. Her only choices were to sell herself or to beg. Either way, the upstanding folks in town would have looked down on her. Besides, selling herself was much more lucrative.

She knew the town despised her and she despised them in return. She vowed never to let anyone hurt her ever again. Her heart grew cold, locked up in a chest where it could no longer be touched. Yet, in the emptiness, her soul longed for more. When she heard about the strange rabbi who went about teaching people how to love, something stirred inside her. Curious, she joined the crowd on the plain to hear Jesus speak and his words broke the chains that bound her heart. When Jesus told the crowd, "Love your enemies. Pray for those who abuse you. If someone takes your coat, give them your shirt as well," she felt he was speaking just to her. For the first time in her life, she glimpsed unconditional love.

And now Jesus was back and she had to see him. She had to repay him in some way—but how? What could a woman like herself offer this man of God? She looked about her room and saw the only thing she had of value—an alabaster jar of ointment, the ointment she used on her clients. She picked up the jar and ran down the street to the home of Simon.

When she got there, Jesus was already reclining at a table inside the courtyard. The table was reserved for those invited to supper, but many others sat or stood around the periphery, hoping to hear what the rabbi had to say. Here, in the presence of Jesus, the woman became filled with emotion and found herself starting to weep out of gratitude and love for what Jesus had done for her.

She crept closer and closer until she came to Jesus' feet. She reached out and touched them and realized that they hadn't been cleaned. Without even thinking, she began to wash them with her tears and dry them with her hair. When they were clean, she kissed them and anointed them with her ointment.

Faintly, in the background, she heard the old familiar recriminations. "Look who's touching the rabbi! Doesn't he know what type of woman she is? She's a sinner!" But Jesus never told her to stop. Instead, he told a story about a man who was forgiven a great debt. Then he told the men at the table, "See this woman? She has done for me what you did not. Her sins, which were many, are now forgiven." With that, Jesus turned to the woman and said, "Your sins are forgiven. You faith has saved you; go in peace."

The woman had felt trapped and imprisoned in a life over which she had no control. She was a sinner—but whose fault was that? It was her husband's fault for abandoning her. It was the law's fault that she didn't have any rights. It was God's fault that all those terrible things kept happening to her. The woman blamed others for her condition and was angry at the whole world. Although she projected strength and defiance, she was really playing the role of a victim. But it was a role she no longer wanted to play. Jesus had shown her another way. He'd shown her that she needed to take the log out of her own eye before she could take the speck out of her neighbor's. Her many sins were not just about sex. They were also about bitterness and the anger. As you take your prayer walk, imagine that you're going to a dinner party with Jesus. This is your chance to finally meet him face-to-face. In one hand you have a list of all the sins you've ever committed. In the other hand you have a list of all the sins others have committed towards you. Ask yourself this: Which list would you rather go over with Jesus and why?

After you've thought about your two lists and are coming to the end of your walk, imagine yourself coming into Jesus' presence. He is looking at you with such love that it almost takes your breath away. He holds out his arms to embrace you. As you extend your arms, you see the two lists in your hands. As Jesus draws near to you, the lists begin to dry up and turn to dust. As the last bits of dust fall from your hands, you look at Jesus and realize that neither list matters. His love forgives all sins. Receive his embrace and hear the words he has for you. "Your faith has saved you," he says. "Go in peace."

The courtyard was buzzing with whispers. All eyes were on Jesus and the woman. Jesus raised his hand to silence the crowd. He looked directly at the woman and said simply, "Your sins are forgiven. Go in peace."

The woman gasped. The sound took her aback. It seemed so loud. She quickly realized that what she heard was not just her own voice. Everyone in the courtyard seemed to gasp right along with her.

The voices started again, but this time they weren't whispering. They sounded shocked and angry. The woman looked questioningly into Jesus' eyes. He smiled, nodded, and gestured toward the doorway.

"Yes, Lord," she said, as she stood up and headed for the outer gate. She stopped for just a moment as she turned back to Jesus and quietly said, "Thank you."

She held her head high as she walked past the people and out into the street. Stepping into the stillness of the night, she felt a freedom she'd never experienced before. Her steps were light. She no longer felt the burden of the past weighing her down. She knew she wasn't the same person who had walked into that courtyard a little while ago. She'd been changed.

When she got home, she gathered all the items that were part of her old life—the make-up, the hair ribbons, the long dangly earrings, the clothes. Tying them all in a bundle, she carried them out to dump.

As she stood at the dump throwing her possessions away, she realized that she was throwing away her old life. She was never again going to treat herself cheaply. She knew what her future would hold. She knew that she'd follow Jesus wherever he led, no matter what. He'd shown her a new way of living, and she decided that included becoming one of his disciples. But she was a woman and a known sinner. Would Jesus want her? She already knew the answer to that. He'd answered that question in the courtyard. Turning her back on her past, she left the dump and went home.

Jesus doesn't look at the outside of a person. He doesn't look at his or her past or what he or she has done. He looks at a person's heart. That's how he sees us. In this woman, he didn't see a prostitute washing his feet. He saw a person with so much love that she performed the most menial of tasks out of humble gratitude.

What is it from your past that still haunts you? Is there something that you know you should let go of, but you just can't seem to do it? Let this walk take you to the dump. Bundle up anything of the old life that's holding you back or tying you to the past. Mentally gather all the items up and stuff them in a big trash bag. Now tie up the bag and get rid of it.

Stop and mentally throw the garbage into the dump. Don't just drop it. Heave it way out into the middle. Now, turn your back on the garbage of the past and walk toward your new life. Sense how much lighter you feel without all that garbage weighing you down.

"Blessed are you, for your sins are forgiven. Go in Peace."

Jairus (Mark 5:22–24, 35–43, Proper 8B)

Jairus knelt by the bedside of his young daughter. Her fever raged beyond control and her breathing had become slow and labored. He wept as he cried out to God for mercy. He prayed the psalms as if they were battering rams against heaven's door. "How long, O Lord? Will you forget me forever? How long will you hide your face?" But each day his daughter grew worse and worse.

The end was very near. As the leader of the synagogue, Jairus had experienced more than his share of death. He'd comforted many who'd lost loved ones, and now he was losing his beloved child. "If only there were something I could do," he cried out. "I would do anything to save my child."

A voice from the back of his head whispered the name "Jesus."

"Jesus? That unauthorized, itinerant rabbi who has the Pharisees in an uproar? I can't go to him. I'm the leader of the synagogue."

"You said you would do anything to save your child. He's healed others. Go to him."

Terror gripped Jairus's heart. Going to Jesus could destroy his reputation, his position, and his career. Jairus looked down at his daughter and realized that there was nothing else to be done. What did any of those things mean to him if he were to lose her? Jairus kissed his daughter's burning forehead and ran out the door to find his last hope.

He ran through the streets of the city looking for Jesus. He asked vendors in the market, shopkeepers, even strangers if they'd seen him. It took him hours, but he finally heard a report that Jesus had sailed across the Sea of Galilee to the far shore. Jairus went into a panic. "Oh God, help me! What if he doesn't come back?" Jairus ran to the docks, determined to rent a boat if he had to.

Reaching the shore, Jairus saw a small crowd of people starting to form. "Could it be?" he thought. "Could it be Jesus?" Yes! It was he. He had found him. Pushing his way through the people, Jairus threw himself at Jesus' feet. "Oh, Lord, please come and touch my daughter. She is near death. Please, Lord, help me please."

Jairus was a man of position and power; it was unseemly for him to grovel at the feet of anyone. To beg was beneath him. But this day, none of that mattered. The only thing that mattered to Jairus was the life of his daughter. He would do whatever was necessary for her to live.

As he knelt there in tears, he felt the hand of Jesus touch his head. "Get up and take me to your daughter," said Jesus. Filled with relief and joy, Jairus started to lead Jesus to his home.

Jairus was a leader of the synagogue; rules, religious law, and tradition governed his life. There was no room for experimentation or guessing. Thinking outside the box was unheard of. His life was neat and organized and in control. All that changed when his twelve-year-old daughter became ill. Rules no longer mattered. Love and life were all that mattered now. Jairus had heard about Jesus. He heard he could heal. He heard he was from God. Jesus was his last hope and he took it.

When we realize that we're not in control of our lives, when all our plans have failed and we have nowhere else to turn, God is waiting for us. It seems that as humans we tend to turn to God as our last hope. But what if we thought of God not as our last hope, but as our first hope? What if we realized that God is all the hope we need?

In this meditation, carry to God one concern you currently have. Don't take all of your concerns—just the one that you need to unload right now. It doesn't even have to be your most desperate situation.

Carry to God one thing that you can honesty let go of. Throw your-self at God's feet. Beg for mercy. Tell God that you can't handle this situation anymore. Ask God to step in and take over. There is nothing more that you can do. Stay in this posture for as long as it takes. Don't get up until you are sure that you can walk away without picking up your concern as you leave.

It's been said that we often live lives of quiet desperation. If desperation means we can't do it on our own, then the statement is partially true. But be quiet about it? No. Wail your prayers to God. Wrestle with angels. Beat on God's door. It's in the engagement that God touches you. It's in answer to your prayer that God sends Jesus. Hold onto God's feet and don't let go. God is the salvation of the desperate.

Relief washed over Jairus when Jesus agreed to follow him home. "Come quickly, Rabbi," he pleaded, as he plowed his way through the swarm. But there was no moving quickly through this crowd. More and more people seemed to come from nowhere. "Please step aside," he pleaded. "My daughter is dying and she needs to see the rabbi."

But no one seemed to hear or care. All Jairus could do was keep moving forward, clearing the path for Jesus. Fear began to creep back into his heart. "Move, please move. We have to hurry!"

Suddenly Jesus stopped. "What is it? What happened?" asked the frightened Jairus.

"Someone grabbed my robe," said Jesus.

The crowd was pressing around Jesus. The disciples reassured Jesus that someone in the crowd must have bumped him. But Jesus didn't move. He looked into the faces of the people standing around him as if he could tell who touched him simply by looking at them.

Jairus began to plead with Jesus. "Sir, it doesn't matter who touched you. Please come before it's too late." Jesus remained silent and still. Suddenly a woman came and threw herself at Jesus' feet. Through her tears, the woman began to speak with Jesus.

All the while, Jairus tried to get Jesus' attention, but to no avail. Jesus was focused on the woman and all Jairus could do was wait.

As he stood waiting, Jairus heard the faint calling of his name. A man was fast approaching, yelling for him, "Master Jairus?" Turning towards the voice, Jairus recognized one of his servants. He ran to the servant, hoping for the best but expecting the worst.

"Master," the servant wept, "there is no need to bother the rabbi any longer. Your daughter is dead." Jairus tore the outer robe of his garments and let out a mighty wail that cut through the murmur of the crowd. Before all the air had even escaped his lungs, Jesus touched Jairus on the shoulder.

"Do not fear. Only believe." With those words, Jesus took a few of his disciples and followed Jairus to his house.

By the time Jairus arrived, the professional mourners had already started. Neighbors and family had gathered outside the house, keeping the proper distance between themselves and the dead body. Before he entered the house, Jesus turned to the mourners and said, "Why do you make a commotion and weep? The child is not dead, merely sleeping."

The mourners scoffed and ridiculed Jesus, but Jesus simply turned and entered the house with Jairus and his wife, with the disciples following behind them. Jesus took the girl by her hand and said to her, "Little girl. Get up!"

Immediately the girl got up and walked around. Jairus picked her up in his arms and held her and kissed her. The fever was gone. She was completely well.

Jesus then told the family to feed her and warned them not to tell anyone about what had happened there that day.

Jairus prayed and God answered. The answer to his prayer was Jesus. God sent Jairus in search of Jesus, and he found him. But before Jesus could cure the little girl, he tarried.

Imagine the emotions swirling inside Jairus—anxiety about reaching home in time, fear at the thought of his daughter's death, anger at the woman who touched Jesus' robe and possibly even at Jesus for the delay. Jairus was worried, anxious, afraid, and angry as he stood next to Jesus, the very answer to his prayer. When it seemed like all was lost and his prayers had gone unanswered, Jesus touched Jairus and said, "Don't be afraid. Have faith."

In your prayer walk today, bring to Jesus any feelings of anxiety, fear, or anger that you have concerning God's timing. As you walk, tell God what you are feeling. Raise your voice to God as the psalmist did.

"O Lord, make haste to help me. . . . Answer me, O Lord. . . . Hear my cry, O God: Listen to my prayer. . . . Answer me when I call, O God of my right. . . . How long, O Lord, will you forget me forever?" (Psalm 13, author's paraphrase).

When you reach the center of the labyrinth or begin returning from your prayer walk, become quiet. The first half of this walk is all about speaking to God. The second half is all about listening to God. You've told God how you feel; now let God minister to those feelings. Allow God the space to work inside you, to show you the fullness of the answer to your prayers. Let God calm your spirit. Listen to Jesus as he tells you not to be afraid. Only believe.

Peter (Matthew 14:22–33, Proper 14A)

Peter and the other eleven disciples struggled against the storm that was driving them off their course. This was the last straw, on a long and difficult day. Jesus had been teaching on the plain of Gennesaret all day. By the time evening approached, the crowd numbered well into the thousands, and the disciples didn't have enough food to feed themselves, let alone enough to share with a multitude. But Jesus had taken what they had and blessed it, and everyone had more than enough to eat. There had been even more food left over than they'd had at the start.

Those close enough to know what had happened began stirring up the crowd, talking about declaring Jesus king. "Surely," they thought, "If he can make food appear out of thin air, he can drive away the Romans!" When Jesus heard what was happening, he told the disciples to get into the boat and sail to Bethsaida. He himself went up on a hilltop to be alone with his heavenly father.

It wasn't long after they'd set off from shore that the wind began to blow. It wasn't a helpful wind—it blew against them and increased in strength. The waves started to beat against the boat, and it seemed that with every oar stroke forward, the storm pushed them two strokes back. What the disciples hoped would be a calm night crossing had turned into an ordeal.

The disciples were frustrated and exhausted. "Why didn't Jesus come with us?" one of them piped up. "We wouldn't be in this mess if Jesus were here."

The eastern sky began to take on a red glow as the dawn approached. Beyond the small boat it was impossible to tell where the sea ended and the storm clouds began. It was that eerie between time when it's neither day nor night. It was just then that Peter noticed something coming toward them out of the darkness. "Could it be another ship?" he asked. As the figure drew closer, it was clear that it was a single human form. One of the disciples cried out, "It's a ghost come to destroy us!" The tired disciples quickly succumbed to fear.

Hearing their cries, the figure called out to the disciples, "Do not fear. It is I." The voice sounded like Jesus. Still not quite sure, Peter stood up and called back, "Master, if it is you, command me to come to you on the water!" Jesus said, "Come."

With his heart pounding, Peter stepped out of the boat. First one foot, then the other. Slowly but steadily, Peter made his way toward

Jesus. Jesus held out his hand as Peter approached. Just as he was lifting his hand in return, Peter glanced back at the other disciples. He didn't realize how far away he was from the boat. It looked so small and the waves pounding against it looked so big. He looked down at his own feet but he couldn't see them for the waves. Panic came upon him like a blast of icy cold air. Before he knew what happened, Peter was in the water. As he bobbed to the surface, he saw Jesus standing above him. Spitting the water out of his mouth, Peter cried out, "Lord, save me!"

Suddenly, a wave came and pushed him down into the sea. As he fell back into the darkness, Peter felt a hand grab his, pulling him to the surface. Gasping for air, he realized that Jesus had him firmly in his grasp. Jesus began pulling Peter out of the water until once again he was standing. Jesus looked at Peter and, with a voice more sad than scolding, said, "You of little faith. Why did you doubt?" Throwing Peter's arm over his shoulder, Jesus helped him back to the boat.

Of course, only Peter would say to Jesus, "Command me to come to you on the water." What a bold request! It was certainly something the impetuous Peter would say. But why? Why would Peter ask Jesus for such a foolish and dangerous test of faith? Whatever Peter was thinking, it must have seemed like a good idea at the time.

But, you see, Peter wasn't really thinking. There was no reason for him to walk out to Jesus. Caught up in the moment, he'd stepped out where he had no business going. It's interesting that Jesus didn't tell him, "No, Peter. Just stay in the boat and I'll be there in a minute." Instead, Jesus said, "Come."

Jesus is always willing for us to step out in faith. We're like little birds on the edge of the nest, looking down at the ground. As soon as we feel ready to take the leap, Jesus is more than happy to say, "Go for it." He wants us to grow in faith and he knows that growth comes through testing. If it isn't scary, a little dangerous, or downright foolish in the world's eyes, then it probably isn't a true test of faith.

Peter was doing fine until he took his eyes off Jesus. Once he lost his focus, he fell into trouble. But Jesus didn't leave him on his own. He didn't stand back and say, "Well, you got yourself into this one— now get yourself out." No! Jesus took Peter by the hand, helped him up, and led him back into the boat. Jesus' words were, "You of little faith. Why did you doubt?" He didn't say, "Don't ever do that again." Jesus was saying, "Trust me. Next time, get it right."

As you walk this meditation, think how you could truly step out in faith. Think of a circumstance in which you could ask Jesus, "Command me to do this, Lord." Whatever it is, imagine walking up to the task. How would it feel? What are your fears? What if your worst fear came true? What would happen? Would you go under and be lost, or would Jesus be there to catch you? Play your worst fears out in your head. Then have Jesus come up to you and help you up. Now play out the scenario as you hope it would turn out. What would be the best thing that could happen? However the situation may turn out, Jesus will be there. Have faith in him. Jesus won't let you fall.

Peter had failed. He wanted to do a great thing. He wanted to be like Jesus. It started out well—he was actually walking on water—but then the reality of the situation got the better of him. Fear replaced faith and Peter fell into the sea.

Now he had to get back into the boat. He was cold, wet, and thoroughly humiliated. Jesus had to practically carry him back. As they were making their way, Peter looked up and saw the other disciples staring at them. "Oh, no," he thought. "I've made a total fool of myself. How will I ever live this down?" Peter wished that he'd never stepped out of the boat in the first place. He felt foolish for daring to emulate Jesus. "Who did I think I was?" he moaned to himself.

When they got to the boat, the disciples looked bewildered, frightened, and, Peter suspected, a little bit amused. Peter's body may have shivered in the cold, but his face burned with embarrassment. The same bold, impetuous Peter, who just moments earlier had stepped out of the boat on his own, now had to be lifted over the bow like a helpless child. Peter cursed himself for being so foolish. "They'll never let me live this one down," he thought to himself.

The wind seemed to stop the moment Jesus set foot inside the boat. The waves ceased and the sun began to appear over the horizon. The red clouds turned to pink, then to golden yellow. The stormy night had passed and it was a brand-new day. The relieved disciples let out cries of joy and thanksgiving. At that moment, all they cared about was praising God and giving thanks to Jesus. Not one word was said to Peter. There were no recriminations—just amazement at what Jesus had done. And Peter, humbled and wet, also gave thanks and praise to God.

As time went by and the story was told over and over again, Peter got his fair share of ribbing. When it came to the part where he fell into the sea, everyone would laugh. Then the laughter would fade, as the disciples would speak of Jesus and how he saved Peter and calmed the storm. They never spoke of Peter's foolishness, but of his bravery for stepping out of the boat. In the eyes of Jesus' followers, there were two heroes in the story—Jesus and Peter.

There isn't anyone in ministry who hasn't failed many times. The ones who say they've never failed have simply never risked stepping out of the boat. Those who don't try never look foolish. Of course, they never accomplish anything either. To become more like Jesus requires you to step out of the boat. It requires you to trust more in God than in the seeming reality of the world around you. Stepping out of the boat is what you're called to do. But sometimes you'll fail. Sometimes you'll start out well but end up in a mess. When that happens, the hardest part is walking back into the community of faith. You'll feel you've let them down. You had good intentions and the best of plans, but it just didn't work out as you had hoped. How will you face them?

Walk this meditation as if you were walking back into church after your specific task or ministry went wrong, when you took a risk and it turned out poorly. Now, imagine walking back into the community of faith. Those who are waiting for you are your friends and colleagues. You see them standing off in the distance. You can feel the anxiety building within you. Now feel the presence of Jesus. Jesus is there, holding you up and giving you support. He is walking with you as you draw closer to your friends. The more anxiety you feel, the more you can lean on Jesus. But you never stop—you keep walking forward until you come face-to-face with them.

Look into the faces of your friends and colleagues. Let them express their gratitude that you even tried. Rejoice that you were brave enough to step out of the boat. Now turn your energy and focus to Jesus. Give him thanks and praise for being with you. Turn over to him all that has happened, both the successes and the failures. Let his love comfort you. Remember, it's better to risk in the name of love than to do nothing at all.

The Rich Young Man (Mark 10:17–27, Proper 23B)

The young man seemed to have everything—good family, position, money. He was admired and envied. "Truly," people often said, "he is blessed by God."

And the young man did feel blessed by God. He was grateful to God for all he'd been given. The young man fulfilled his sacred obligations and did all that the law and the prophets required of him. Yet he wasn't completely happy. There was something missing. He had no idea what it could be, but a nagging emptiness kept him restless.

Then the young man began hearing about Jesus of Nazareth. Whenever he heard Jesus was traveling near his town, he went to hear him teach. He was touched by Jesus' words in a way that seemed to fill the emptiness. One day he resolved to do something about it.

He decided to go to Jesus and ask the secret to finding the kingdom of God.

As the young man walked into town, he heard that Jesus was preparing to leave. His mission suddenly became more urgent. He ran to the center of town where the synagogue was located, hoping to catch up with Jesus. Upon seeing Jesus and his disciples, the young man ran up to Jesus and knelt at his feet. "Good teacher," he asked, "What must I do to inherit eternal life?"

Jesus looked at him with some puzzlement. "Why do you call me good? No one is good but God alone." The young man's face flushed with embarrassment.

Jesus smiled at the young man and beckoned him to stand. Looking into his eyes, Jesus said, "You know the commandments: 'You shall not murder; You shall not commit adultery; You shall not steal; You shall not bear false witness; You shall not defraud; Honor your father and mother.'"

The young man replied, "Teacher, I have kept all these things since my youth."

Jesus knew the young man was telling the truth. Jesus also knew the young man's heart. He knew its emptiness. Jesus also knew the fears that kept the young man from entering fully into the kingdom of God. With the loving tenderness of a skilled surgeon, Jesus cut to the young man's very core. "There is one thing you must do," he said. "You must sell what you own, give it to the poor, then come follow me."

The words of Jesus cut to the young man's heart like a searing knife. The air seemed to be sucked right out of his lungs. Panic exploded throughout his entire body. In that instant, everything stopped as if he had been struck dead. The young man gasped and, with the inrushing of air, his brain began to scramble to bring some rationale to what was happening. "I can't. I can't," he mumbled. Jesus only looked at him. Not with contempt, but with pity. Jesus offered the young man the answer to his longing, but the young man was unable to receive it.

How many times have you looked at the lives of others with admiration and envy? Did you wish you had their life and they had yours? What about your own life? Are there times when you come across to the world as having it all together? Have others ever looked at you with envy? The difference is that you know the empty places in your own heart. You know that sometimes the image is just that, an image, and not the way you truly feel. As you look at others, you can't see their emptiness, pain, or longing. But they are there.

Have you ever had surgery or undergone medical tests? You knew the doctors were there to make you well. What needed to be done was for your own good and was life giving, but that didn't stop you from being scared. The prospect of going under the knife or being probed isn't something we look forward to. But the purpose of this prayer walk is to encourage you to do just that. Walk to Jesus in much the same way you would walk into the hospital or the doctor's office. You trust Jesus to heal you. You know that he only wants what is good for you. You also know that he will open you up and look deep inside you—not to hurt you, but to heal the brokenness that lies within.

As you walk, let your feelings come to the surface. Express any fear or anxiety you may have. Be honest. After you've gotten that out of the way, listen to what Jesus has to say to you. He is the great physician and he knows exactly what you need to do to enter fully into the kingdom of God. Accept his diagnosis and his course of treatment. Don't be like the rich young man and run away. Stay in the presence of Jesus. Draw your strength from him. Jesus will give you the power to overcome your fears. In Christ, you will be healed.

The young man had everything the world could offer. He wanted the one thing that this world can't provide—eternal life. So he ran after Jesus to find the key to the kingdom of God. He ran to Jesus, knelt before him, and asked for the secret to spiritual success. He demanded, "What must I do?"

Jesus' response was unfathomable to the young man. "Sell everything, give it to the poor, and come follow me."

The young man was bewildered. How could Jesus ask such a thing? The young man felt that his wealth was proof of God's blessing on his righteousness, a sign of God's favor.

He thought about his family and how they were accorded places of honor wherever they went. He couldn't imagine walking away, not only from his position, but also from who he was. In his mind, Jesus was asking him to leave behind his very identity. That's why the story refers to the man not by name, but by position—a rich young ruler.

The rich young man walked away. His wealth and his position were too much to give. The gospel tells us he walked away in grief because he had many possessions. The cost of discipleship was too high. Though he wanted the benefits of a holy life, he couldn't let go of his worldly life. His decision was an issue of faith and trust. He trusted in his wealth instead of having faith in God. His desire was genuine and his motives were pure, but he lacked the faith necessary to do what Jesus asked of him.

As you walk this path today, offer to God those times when you lacked the faith to do what you knew God wanted of you. Reflect on the crossroads you've faced. Look back at the times when you picked the easier, more familiar path. Do you feel any grief over your decision? If so, offer it to God. Express it and then let it go. Give it God and let God heal it.

We never hear about the rich young man again. We don't know what happened to him. He could have gone through his entire life without ever changing. It is also possible that after some time and prayerful reflection, he conquered his fears and became a true disciple of Jesus. No matter how many times you have taken the easy path in the past, each time you come to a crossroad, you can make the choice once again to put your trust in God. It's what you do the next time that counts. Now, have faith. Step out and follow Jesus.

A Pattern for a Simple Finger Labyrinth

Copy the pattern and enlarge if necessary. Place the pattern under a light piece of fabric. Trace over the pattern with a fabric marker or fabric paint. NOTE: Fabric paint works better because it allows you to feel the shape of the labyrinth with your finger as you go along.

CPSIA information can be obtained at www.ICGtesting.com
Printed in the USA
LVOW06s0255301215

468377LV00002B/8/P